Bridging Case Conceptualization, Assessment, and Intervention

Bridging Case Conceptualization, Assessment, and Intervention

Scott T. Meier

State University of New York, Buffalo

SAGE Publications
International Educational and Professional Publisher
Thousand Oaks ■ London ■ New Delhi

For information:

Sage Publications, Inc.
2455 Teller Road
Thousand Oaks, California 91320
E-mail: order@sagepub.com

Sage Publications Ltd.
6 Bonhill Street
London EC2A 4PU
United Kingdom

Sage Publications India Pvt. Ltd.
B-42 Panchsheel Enclave
Post Box 4109
New Delhi 110 017 India

Printed in the United States of America

Library of Congress Cataloging-in-Publication Data

Meier, Scott T., 1955-
Bridging case conceptualization, assessment, and intervention / Scott T. Meier.
    p. cm.
Includes bibliographical references and index.
ISBN 0-7619-2368-3
1. Psychotherapy. 2. Psychotherapy-Evaluation. I. Title.
RC480.5 .M365 2002
616.89´14—dc21   2002013029

02   03   04   05   10   9   8   7   6   5   4   3   2   1

Acquiring Editor:	Margaret H. Seawell
Editorial Assistant:	Alicia Carter
Production Editor:	Claudia A. Hoffman
Copy Editor:	Jamie Robinson
Cover Designer:	Michelle Lee

CONTENTS

————•◦•————

PREFACE

A ttempts to bridge the science and practice of clinical work in mental health have a long history (Hess & Mullen, 1995; Pepinsky & Pepinsky, 1954; Stricker & Trierweiler, 1995). Eldridge (1993), for example, noted that accountability (i.e., outcome assessment) had been proposed as the central issue confronting social workers during the 1970s; counseling educators have expressed concerns about students' ability to conceptualize clients for decades (Holloway & Wolleat, 1980; Nelson & Neufeldt, 1998). Yet many observers (e.g., Goldman, 1972) conclude that a science-practice integration has failed or at least failed to meet expectations. Potential explanations include:

1. The science-practice link has been strained because of the different purposes of scientists and practitioners. Researchers are typically concerned with discovering general laws, whereas practitioners focus on helping specific cases that consist of individuals, groups, and families (e.g., Fensterheim & Raw, 1996; Hess & Mullen, 1995; Stricker & Trierweiler, 1995).

2. Many students in the helping professions enter graduate school with vocational interests that are socially oriented and unrelated to research activities (Kahn & Scott, 1997). Beginning students, for example, often express a stronger desire to learn the what and how (i.e., techniques) of clinical work than the why; graduates in the helping professions seldom conduct or publish research. Expecting such individuals to change their vocational interests and abilities is unrealistic.

3. Clinicians have been resistant to evaluation efforts because of the additional workload and the potential for critical feedback involved (Nugent, Sieppert, & Hudson, 2001). Issues of accountability and effectiveness often hold more interest for administrators, funding agencies, and researchers than

they do for clinicians. Thus, scientific methods have been perceived as having little to offer clinicians except negative consequences.

4. Scientific methods and clinical practice are typically taught in separate courses and seldom completely integrated (Meier, 1999; Stoltenberg, Kashubeck-West, Biever, Patterson, & Welch, 2000). Chwalisz (2001) noted that "the scientist-practitioner model, as currently enacted in psychology training programs, has not built a sufficient relationship between science and practice" (p. 265). Many training programs appear to assume that if graduate students receive separate courses in research design, testing and assessment, and reviews of counseling research, they will naturally integrate this information into their work with clients. My experience as a student and faculty member is that this is usually not the case: Many students differentiate research and practice into separate domains.

This book approaches the science-practice problem by focusing explicitly on the links between case conceptualization, assessment, and analysis of intervention effects during clinical work. Observing the professional behaviors of neurosurgeons, Gladwell (1996) noted that "the complexity and mystery of the brain has . . . led to a culture that rewards intuition, and has thus convinced each neurosurgeon that [his or her] own experience is as valid as anyone else's" (p. 39). Like neurosurgeons, clinicians conducting psychotherapy typically receive little systematic feedback about the effects of their work and make many of their decisions intuitively. The approach described in this book attempts to present a balance between questioning and supporting clinical intuition by making clinicians' thoughts, decisions, and judgments explicit, and then checking them against other kinds of information (see Berman, 1997; O'Brien, 1995). By integrating this structured approach directly into the content of clinical, theoretical, and practicum courses, faculty can increase the likelihood that student clinicians will increase their confidence in using more systematic methods and thus actually use them (Meier, 1999).

The most basic reason for investing in such an integrative approach is improving clinical outcomes. Failure to conceptualize and monitor treatment may be one of the contributing factors to treatment failure (Clark, 1999). In addition, by closely linking case conceptualization and assessment data with intervention decisions, students and clinicians can (a) be introduced to a standard of practice that moves beyond an eclectic, flying-by-the-seat-of-your-pants approach to therapy and (b) better understand why counseling is ineffective with some individuals and thus have a basis for adjusting treatment in those instances. A commitment to an integrative approach that increases professional reflection should also foster clinicians' professional development (Ronnestand & Skovholt, 2001; Skovholt & Ronnestand, 1995).

Four basic themes form the foundation of this integrative approach. First, Lazarus (1971, p. xi) cautioned clinicians "not to forget the obvious fact that every individual is unique, and to tailor . . . therapy accordingly" (cited in Gottman & Leiblum, 1974). Many psychotherapy theories and clinical measures, however, treat clients as if they were largely interchangeable and not individual interpreters and creators of meaning. Although case conceptualization, clinical assessment, and intervention are built on nomothetic theories, they work best when focused on the relatively unique, *idiographic* aspects of each client.

Second, this integrative approach differs from traditional methods of teaching counseling and psychotherapy in its emphasis on the inclusion of *assessment data* in the intervention process. For example, while many counseling texts provide information related to counseling process and intervention, and some explicitly relate this information to client conceptualization, few thoroughly and systematically connect conceptualization and intervention with assessment. Assessment tends to be taught in separate courses on measurement, intelligence testing, and personality testing. The extent to which assessment is integrated into the therapeutic process often depends upon the judgment and background of a particular supervisor in a practicum setting. In fact, the mental health professions appear to be lagging behind medicine and education in their use of assessment data as feedback in the intervention process (see Cross & Angelo, 1988; Mark et al., 1991).

Third, *structured feedback* is critical to learning for both students and practicing clinicians. Experience becomes helpful when we have "systematic procedures for learning from our failures as well as our successes" (Gottman & Leiblum, 1974, p. 9). When clinicians closely examine the set of outcomes experienced by each client, they often find evidence of both success and failure. Thus, analysis of clinically relevant data is key to learning about and improving work with individual clients.

Fourth, this approach focuses on the application of *scientific methods*, as contrasted with the exclusive use of specific theoretical knowledge or empirical results. The methods and procedures described in this book are transtheoretical in that they can potentially be applied by clinicians of any particular school of counseling and psychotherapy. The descriptions and examples provided here include a variety of modalities (e.g, individual, group, family) and therapeutic orientations (e.g., social learning, multicultural). Instructors should modify and employ these concepts with whatever therapeutic approaches they prefer, as well as adapt and introduce their particular techniques for case conceptualization, clinical assessment, and analysis of intervention effects.

This book will be useful to graduate students in clinical fields, and postgraduate clinicians may benefit from a review of these concepts. Introductory courses in counseling theory (including theories of personality, psychopathology, and psychotherapy), measurement and assessment, and qualitative or quantitative analysis will help the reader make sense of these chapters. These materials are intended as an extension of or sequel to class texts, to be used in psychotherapy, counseling, and practical classes where the instructor wishes to bring scientific methods into the discussion of clinical issues. With its emphasis on concepts and procedure, the book's primary intended use is as a manual; those looking for discussions of philosophical foundations should consult sources such as Trierweiler and Stricker (1998). Because the focus of the book is the *integration* of conceptualization, assessment, and analysis of intervention effects, the treatment of each of these areas is necessarily brief; references are cited in each chapter for sources that provide a deeper discussion. When referring to the counselor or therapist, I prefer to use the word *clinician,* as it "is a general term used to refer to individuals who have obtained, or are in the process of obtaining, professional training in psychology, counseling, education, or social work departments at universities, medical centers, or training institutions" (Berman, 1997, p. xi). Given the diverse potential readership of the book, terms like *psychotherapy* and *counseling* are employed interchangeably.

The book consists of six chapters. Chapter 1 provides an introduction to the key elements of conceptualization, assessment, and analysis, as well as a more thorough rationale for their integration. Chapter 2 introduces and guides the clinician through the steps necessary to select (a) process elements related to client etiology and intervention and (b) outcome elements for multiple and selected problems. In Chapter 3, the focus shifts to how to assess these process and outcome elements; the presentation includes an overview of assessment methods (including idiographic and behavioral assessment), construct explication, psychometric principles, guidelines for method selection, the use of baselines, and examples. Chapter 4 presents basic graphical, qualitative, and quantitative analytic techniques that can be used to address questions related to outcome, conceptualization, and assessment. Chapter 5 addresses common problems in conceptualization, idiographic assessment, and analysis, while Chapter 6 includes possible future directions for science-practice efforts in the helping professions.

Portions of this book are based on Meier (1994, 1999); more detailed descriptions of teaching methods related to this material are in Meier (1999), and descriptions of measurement and assessment issues can be found in Meier (1994). Client and therapist names and characteristics have been altered to protect confidentiality; because the purpose of the data presented in this book is teaching, not research, some data have also been altered to protect confidentiality. I would like to thank the many graduate students (particularly Caroline Baltzer, Julie Nettina, Benson Hendricks-Hoffman, and Beth Wahlig) who provided creative (but sometimes uncited, to protect confidentiality) examples of clinical models and analytic displays. Finally, I would like to thank my graduate assistants, the latest including Ron Beebe, Benson Hendricks-Hoffman, Christine Messmer, Julie Nettina, and Erin Steck, for their considerable assistance and helpful feedback.

— *Scott T. Meier, Ph.D.*
stmeier@acsu.buffalo.edu
www.acsu.buffalo.edu/~stmeier
University at Buffalo
August 19, 2002

INTRODUCTION

———•◦•———

W hy attempt to integrate case conceptualization, clinical assessment, and analysis of psychotherapy effects into the clinical process? Because such a linkage can begin to solve several difficult problems in contemporary clinical work. The first is the issue of accountability: At no other time have clinicians been under such pressure to produce data supporting their work. Managed care companies and other settings where managed care philosophies have been adopted frequently require clinicians to employ outcome measures; few of the involved parties, however, are aware of the considerable validity issues associated with commonly used measures. Second, the literature on clinical judgment indicates that clinician errors can be frequent and substantial, yet the field has reached little consensus about procedures for detecting and correcting such errors. Third, treatment failure rates have been estimated in the literature as between 10% and 30%; however, clinicians have no systematic methods for identifying or responding to clients' lack of progress. Finally, while a science-practice philosophy is frequently espoused as a standard in clinical fields, how this philosophy is implemented often depends more on the skill and intentions of individual instructors than any other factor.

Based on a philosophy of integrating scientific methods into practice, the goal of this book is to help clinicians make explicit connections between case conceptualization, clinical assessment, analysis of intervention-related data, and interventions with clients (see Beutler & Harwood, 2000; Persons, 1989). Instead of seeing treatment as consisting only of the interventions and interactions that take place in therapy sessions (or in homework), the approach described

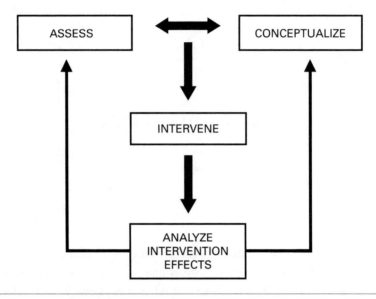

Figure 1.1   Sequential Relations Among Assessment, Conceptualization,
Intervention, and Analysis of Intervention Effects

here makes conceptualization, assessment, and analysis *integral components of any treatment.* This book can be conceived of as a treatment manual, but one that encompasses more information than what is commonly perceived of as therapeutic interventions.

As shown in Figure 1.1, the desired process can be seen as a *flexible feedback loop* that consists of

a conceptualization and corresponding selection of clinical measures for a specific client that

leads to a selected intervention (or interventions)

whose effects are examined empirically,

with those results then fed back to the clinician (and perhaps, the client) so that the interventions (and perhaps, the conceptualization and assessment) can be reconsidered and adapted if necessary.

Clinicians can begin their work prepared with ideas about how to intervene and assess the effects of the intervention (Meier, 1999). Analyses of the resulting data can be fed back into conceptualization, assessment, and intervention procedures to increase the likelihood that the clinical work will be successful.

This and other types of feedback loops can provide clinicians with useful information with which to create treatment plans and adjust therapy as circumstances change (Haynes, 1993; Howard, Moras, Brill, Martinovich, & Lutz, 1996; Lambert, 1998; Lambert et al., 2001; Mark et al., 1991; Palmer, 1986). Often neglected in theories of psychotherapy, feedback is a fundamental determinant of performance: No improvement is likely without it, and deterioration occurs when it is withdrawn (see, e.g., Bilodeau & Bilodeau, 1961, cited in Gentile, 1990). The lack of systematic feedback in psychotherapy may partially account for the presence of clinical judgment errors frequently reported in the research literature. Gottman and Leiblum (1974) recommended that clinicians obtain a "continuous monitoring of progress toward goals with the data used as feedback to make decisions about the effectiveness of intervention components of the treatment program" (p. v). Some of the most successful psychotherapeutic approaches depend heavily on feedback from comprehensive clinical assessments (e.g., Paul & Menditto, 1992).

Lambert and colleagues (2001) recently demonstrated the positive effects of feedback with clients who fail to make progress in therapy. Using the Outcome Questionnaire (OQ-45) with 609 university counseling center clients, this study examined the effect of two factors: Feedback versus no feedback to therapist, and clients making therapeutic progress versus those who were not (on OQ scores). Feedback consisted of graphs and progress markers, colored dots that indicated whether the client was functioning in the normal range (of OQ scores), showing an adequate rate of change, showing an inadequate rate of change, or failing to make any progress. Lambert and colleagues found support for the major hypothesis of the study: OQ scores at termination were higher for clients who initially were not making progress, but whose therapist was receiving feedback, compared to clients who were not making progress and whose therapist received no feedback. In fact, the latter group worsened over time. Lambert and colleagues also noted that the effect size comparing the difference between the two groups' posttest scores was larger than that found in studies comparing different types of psychotherapy.

Summarizing the results of Lambert and colleagues (2001) and Lambert and colleagues (in press), Gray and Lambert (2001) concluded:

The studies found that clinicians are not effective in gauging patient response to treatment, especially in early treatment sessions. However, when they are provided with feedback on poor treatment response, they develop a perspective on their patient's clinical progress that enables them to recalibrate treatment and make a substantial impact on improvement rates. . . . The major finding of the studies is that the use of feedback provides information that gives the clinician a perspective on change that cannot be derived from clinical intuition alone, and that this feedback enhances outcomes with at-risk clients. The magnitude of improvement in outcomes is greater than that found when clinicians apply a specialized (manual-based) modality or follow treatment protocols. (p. 26)

The integration of conceptualization, assessment, and analysis of intervention effects also presents an opportunity to remedy problems created by an overreliance on any one of these areas alone. When theorizing about clients (i.e., the armchair approach), the temptation is to believe that what we think about something actually constitutes the whole of that thing. Collecting and analyzing data about our conceptualizations tempers overconfidence by providing corrective feedback. Similarly, we may be tempted to believe that using data alone (the empirical approach) reflects clinical reality, forgetting the always-present multiple influences (i.e., sources of error) on those data. Thus, conceptualization and assessment are most useful when used in combination: Assessment produces data useful for evaluating conceptualization, while conceptualization of clinical and methodological factors assists in an improved interpretation of assessment data.

For a number of reasons, however, implementing such a clinical feedback procedure can be difficult and complex. Clinicians think about their clients, at least implicitly, in terms of the causes of their problem and the desired outcomes of the intervention. Although those conceptualizations can provide a useful map for proceeding with clients, clinicians' thoughts and beliefs can also be misleading. Even experienced clinicians can make errors in judgment and remain overconfident about the validity of those judgments (Spengler, Strohmer, Dixon, & Shivy, 1995). For example, clinicians may focus on only one event or problem in a client's life, missing other important influences (Mattaini, 1993; Spengler & Strohmer, 1994).

Contemporary practices in clinical assessment represent another source of difficulty in implementing a feedback loop. Most clinicians produce qualitative information (i.e., case notes) and a few collect quantitative data (e.g., outcome assessments) as part of their routine record keeping. Often with the prodding of managed care companies or other funding sources, agencies and individual clinicians employ tests such as the Outcome Questionnaire (OQ-45) or the Beck Depression Inventory-2 (BDI-2) in an attempt to measure and document client progress. At present, however, nomothetic test results alone are generally too imprecise to guide decisions about psychological interventions for an individual client (Cronbach & Gleser, 1965; Meier, 1994; Paul, Mariotto, & Redfield, 1986). In addition, many published instruments are too lengthy for practical use and provide data clinicians consider of little treatment relevance (Bickman et al., 2000).

Finally, many clinicians have little experience with the process of integrating conceptualization, assessment, and intervention explicitly. Despite suggestions that such an integration be taught in introductory courses, assessment courses, and clinical practica (see, e.g., Heppner et al., 1992; Spengler et al., 1995), rarely do students combine conceptualization, assessment, and analysis into an integrated whole and apply the resulting knowledge with actual clients (Meier, 1999). Part of the problem may be that the typical student selected into the helping professions often possesses greater interest in developing the helping relationship than in learning the entire repertoire of skills needed for effective therapy. And while graduate training in psychology produces an increase in reasoning abilities (Lehman, Lempert, & Nisbett, 1988), instructors should not assume that teaching about research methodology or statistical analysis in separate courses means that all students will automatically apply such knowledge in practice situations. Much learning and its application appear to be situation and domain specific (Gentile, 1990; Lehman et al., 1988). Transfer of new learning, such as scientific methods into clinical practice, is enhanced when learners are encouraged to identify and employ underlying principles in new contexts.

Rather than assuming students will transfer their research training to practice settings, the scientific components of conceptualization, assessment, and analysis models should be integrated directly into counseling and practicum courses. What clinical educators want to encourage is the idea of *praxis*, "ensuring that opportunities for the interplay between action and reflection are available in a balanced way for students. Praxis means that curricula are not studied in some kind of artificial isolation, but that ideas, skills, and insights learned in a classroom are tested and experienced in real life" (Brookfield, 1990, p. 50).

BUILDING ON TRADITIONAL NOMOTHETIC APPROACHES

While *nomothetic* methods focus on what always occurs or is present across all persons, *idiographic* approaches emphasize the fundamental importance of attending to unique aspects of individuals and their life situations (Pervin, 1984). Nomothetic and idiographic perspectives are typically contrasted as opposites, yet they can also be seen as complementary approaches with different purposes.

Theorists, researchers, and test developers typically take a nomothetic approach when they attempt to develop universal laws of behavior or investigate the usefulness of different psychotherapies for specific problems. In addition, nomothetic measures have proven useful for three specific purposes in clinical contexts (see Haynes, Spain, & Oliveira, 1993). First, in program evaluation and outcome research, nomothetic tests can provide data for an overall indication of whether or not change has occurred in treatment and control groups (see Meier, 1997, 1998; Davis & Meier, 2001). Second, if you wish to predict a discrete event or outcome (i.e., a criterion such as GPA in college study) for a group of individuals and to have a method found to be predictive of that event (e.g., a test such as the SAT), the best choice is to give the test and predict statistically (e.g., Wiggins, 1973). For example, if a client wishes to know which occupations she or he will find most satisfying, a vocational interest test will typically be more useful than clinical intuition alone. Finally, nomothetic tests can be used to generate hypotheses about a particular client. The clinician can examine high scale scores as well as individual items endorsed by clients on tests such as the Outcome Questionnaire-45 (OQ-45), Beck Depression Inventory-2 (BDI-2), or Minnesota Multiphasic Personality Inventory-2 (MMPI-2) to identify issues of most relevance to that particular client.

Clinicians might be most effective when they begin therapy with knowledge of nomothetic theories, research findings, and test results that they then tailor for use with individual clients. This, in effect, is what appears to happen during most psychotherapy, but it often happens in a haphazard way (Watkins, 1997). This book emphasizes a more structured approach to conceptualization, assessment, and intervention with particular clients. As shown below and in the following chapters, the approach described here attempts to increase the rigor of the idiographic method (see Chwalisz, 2001).

Idiographic Conceptualization

Traditional academic approaches to studying, learning, and teaching about psychotherapy and counseling emphasize a nomothetic perspective that focuses on how psychotherapy theories (and research evaluating those theories) apply to all people. On the other hand, clinicians typically want to help a particular individual who possesses some relatively unique aspects. Kazdin (2000), discussing the results of meta-analyses, noted that "the metric makes sense for specific research purposes but tells nothing whatsoever about what happens to individuals who receive a particular treatment" (p. 213). An idiographic approach can help the clinician understand a specific person in at least two ways often neglected by nomothetic theories (Allport, 1937, 1942). First, contexts and situations influence behavior, and discussions of the types (e.g., family, work) and the effects of situations are usually important to creating a useful case conceptualization (Stricker & Trierweiler, 1995). Second, particular clients will perceive and make sense of identical events in different ways (Meier & Davis, 2001). The clinician's knowledge of how clients create and find meaning is thus also critical for understanding and intervening with individual clients.

Most graduate programs in the helping professions include at least one general theories course that provides an overview of the important contemporary approaches to psychotherapy. Intervention theories provide information relevant to the identification of important constructs, and their cause-effect relationships, relevant to clinical work (e.g., Mattaini, 1997). These theories, however, often provide little guidance with regard to useful definitions of important constructs; how, when, and on whom the constructs should be measured; and how the constructs might interact (see Lipsey & Pollard, 1989). Similarly, reviews of outcome studies provide broad findings that indicate the effectiveness of most forms of counseling and psychotherapy (e.g., Smith & Glass, 1977). For example, Dobson's (1989) meta-analysis found that cognitive therapy helped to alleviate depression, while Bednar and Kaul (1994) concluded that experiential group interventions are more effective than no treatment or placebos.

Even with an intervention known to be effective, on average, with a specific problem—an empirically validated or supported treatment—individual clients will vary substantially in their response to that treatment, particularly over time (Barlow, Hayes, & Nelson, 1984; Brown & Barlow, 1995; Quayle & Moore,

1998). Streiner (1998) noted that "even though some treatments have been shown to be efficacious in clinical trials, there is no guarantee that they are effective with a specific patient" (p. 737). The effectiveness of interventions based on standardized or manualized treatments may still depend on the clinician's understanding of a client's unique processes and functioning (Layden, Newman, Freeman, & Morse, 1993; Needleman, 1999). For example, clients may present with different types of beliefs or have problems triggered by different situations. As Stricker and Trierweiler (1995) noted, it is "the contextual factors that make application so complex" (pp. 996-997). When employing empirically supported approaches, the clinician must still judge how the approach should be adapted to the particular client (Eifert, Schulte, Zvolensky, Lejuez, & Lau, 1997; Elliott, 1998; Persons & Silberschatz, 1998).

Also, many clients present with multiple problems that require adjustment to a treatment package. Many studies of psychotherapy outcome have also ignored the effects of gender and culture (see McGuire, 1999), thereby making their generalization to non-White populations even more problematic. Finally, outcome studies often provide little information about why or how the therapies work. In a statement that applies to most forms of psychotherapy, Bednar and Kaul (1994) concluded that "it is scientifically awkward to maintain that group treatments work without specifying the curative factors that account for this success" (p. 632).

When done systematically, the process of case conceptualization encourages a clinician to consider important influences on a particular client as well as how and when to describe and measure those influences (see Lipsey & Pollard, 1989). More specifically, representing those factors in a graph or figure can help clinicians cope with their complexity. As Mattaini (1993) explains, using graphics to visualize the processes and outcomes of individual clients can help us "make sense of it, to clarify not only one issue at a time but ever-changing transactions among persons, systems, and issues" (p. 2). By helping clinicians to organize complex information and identify patterns that have implication for treatment and the assessment of treatment effects, graphical conceptualizations can improve clinicians' comprehension and recall of clinical data (see Mattaini, 1993).

Idiographic Assessment

Idiographic measures are designed to assess how an individual makes sense of or uniquely manifests a construct of interest. For that reason, idiographic clinical assessment can potentially provide a level of precision beyond that provided by nomothetic measures; thus, idiographic assessments are likely to make better predictions of an individual's behavior than are nomothetic tests (Lamiel, 1981; Shadel, Niaura, & Abrams, 2000).

The use of nomothetic tests is based on the assumption that each person interprets test items and instructions in largely the same way. This fallacy can be demonstrated by a simple experiment. Choose any brief self-report instrument (e.g., the State-Trait Anxiety Inventory; Spielberger, Gorsuch, & Lushene, 1970) and administer it to any group of 15 to 20 individuals. After the items are completed, ask these individuals to explain how they interpreted each item and the basis on which they answered the items. For many items, a few (but usually more than one) basic meanings will be agreed upon by most of the group; for a more complex item, multiple interpretations will be offered. It is also likely that a few individuals in this group will account for most of the unusual interpretations. The purpose of this experiment is to demonstrate that nomothetic tests contain language that individuals must interpret. The result of this is that when individuals encounter test items that are even minimally ambiguous or multidimensional, they will interpret the constructs differently and therefore interact with the testing instrument in unique ways (Kahn & Meier, 1999, 2001; Schwarz, 1999).

Nomothetic tests have limitations in clinical situations with individual clients (Goldman, 1972; Hayes, Nelson, & Jarrett, 1987; Hummel, 1999). Nomothetic tests are typically developed for the purpose of detecting individual differences (usually of psychological traits) and making subsequent predictions of future events, not for detecting the specific effects of treatments with individuals (Meier, 1994, 1997, 1998). Cone (1988) summarized this problem:

> Norm-referenced instruments, useful as they are for describing differences among individuals, are, by their very nature, not sensitive enough to be used to evaluate the intervention programs typical of behavior change specialists. . . . They are constructed in ways that render them insensitive to the kinds of changes likely to be produced by individual intervention programs. (p. 55)

Likewise, brief, global measures such as the Global Assessment of Functioning scale (GAF; American Psychiatric Association, 1994), perhaps the most widely used outcome measure, can be employed as general indices of change but provide little specific information relevant for implementing or modifying therapy with particular clients. Contemporary GAF ratings are often suspect because managed care companies may set a GAF threshold for authorizing services; clinicians quickly ascertain this number and provide the appropriate rating to ensure services for their clients. Not surprisingly, Bickman and colleagues' (2000) survey of practicing clinicians found that they considered the information provided by global measures of outcome among the information they least desired.

Similarly, Haynes and colleagues (1993) suggested that because there can be many possible causes for a single problem, diagnosis is a necessary but insufficient condition for identifying causal variables. They concluded that:

> Although diagnosis or problem behavior specification can be helpful in defining a field of possible causes, they are usually insufficient to identify the specific causal variables for an individual client. A vast research literature supports the conclusion that there are multiple potential causes for most behavior problems. (p. 283)

Because two clients can be diagnosed with the same disorder but exhibit different levels of impairment, Wiger (1999) noted that a diagnosis itself does not determine the level of mental health services needed. Diagnosis also becomes problematic when (a) clients receive a diagnosis at the beginning of treatment that does not change despite additional, clinically relevant information (as often happens when diagnosis is done at intake and not reexamined during the course of treatment), and (b) the diagnosis has little or no specific relation to the subsequent intervention (as occurs when clinicians of one psychotherapeutic school employ that school's approach with all clients regardless of diagnosis).

Despite a long history of constructing idiographic measures for clinical purposes (e.g., DeWitt, Kaltreider, Weiss, & Horowitz, 1983; Malan, 1959), no consensus has been reached on a standard methodology. What many clinical researchers agree is needed are idiographic measures that are sensitive to the specific behaviors of individual clients likely to change during the course of treatment (Bickman et al., 2000; Cone, 1988; Kiresuk, Smith, & Cardillo, 1994; Mash & Hunsley, 1993). These assessments should also be brief and relatively inexpensive (as a result of being focused on the targets of change), treatment sensitive (and thus indicators of progress and failure in therapy), and easily modified (or dropped, if treatment goals change).

ASSUMPTIONS AND VALUES

Clinicians should be able to provide an account of their activities so that judgments can be made about the adequacy of those activities and about how current practices could be improved. This view of accountability differs from that of some "public and private sector purchasers of mental health services [who] see measurement of client outcomes as a form of accounting rather than as a way to improve services" (Bickman et al., 2000, p. 72). Accountability where clinicians are compared to each other in terms of effectiveness, client satisfaction, or cost may very well preclude improvement of services because clinicians in such a system can distort their performances and their clients' functioning to make the best impression (Davis & Meier, 2001). Because client problems have multiple causes, some outside of psychotherapeutic influence, clinicians should not be held accountable for the improvement of each client (Kazdin, 1999). Kazdin (1999) concluded that clinicians cannot be "held responsible for achieving the therapeutic changes that all parties involved would like. They can, however, be held accountable for careful evaluation and for informed decision-making" (p. x)

A major drawback to the approach described in this book involves the required resources of time, effort, and money. Professional standards typically mandate minimal requirements in these areas, usually including an intake assessment (and subsequent, loosely specified case conceptualization and treatment planning), progress notes, and outcome assessment. In an era of scarce resources and increased workload resulting from factors such as the managed care of mental health (Davis & Meier, 2001), the more extensive effort needed to do systematic conceptualization, assessment, and analysis may be challenging.

I offer three suggestions in this regard. First, do as little conceptualization, assessment, and analysis as necessary (see Meier & Letsch, 2000). Performance of these tasks should enhance, not detract from, the needed provision of services. Second, consider what is necessary in the context of each particular client. In most educational and clinical settings, norms exist about the usual type and amounts of conceptualization, assessment, and analysis. Third, the concept of treatment failure can be utilized to determine when to expend the additional resources required to perform systematic conceptualization, assessment and analysis. That is, when a client fails to make progress, additional effort is warranted; this criterion will be discussed in greater depth in coming chapters.

Clearly, a tension will frequently exist between the desire to implement a science-based approach, such as the one described here, and the realities of clinical practice. The best resolution of this tension may be a philosophy of *flexible systematics* where a structured approach to conceptualization, assessment, and analysis is tailored to benefit the client while considering the larger clinical context. A clinician with a large caseload during a particular time period, for example, might perform only a minimal clinical assessment (e.g., use of the GAF for outcome measurement). Conversely, evidence of treatment failure with a client may indicate that additional resources need to be allocated to conduct a thorough case conceptualization, clinical assessment, and analysis of clinical data to suggest alternative interventions.

Given the complexity of the conceptualization, assessment, analysis, and intervention tasks inherent in many psychotherapy cases (Garb, 1998), it also makes sense to value tentativeness and humility about the questions and answers pursued in clinical work. Certainty in these domains is not a realistic goal; errors in conceptualization, assessment, and analysis may be best viewed as feedback relevant to improving future efforts. Given the relative youth of the fields of psychotherapy and psychotherapy research, it also appears reasonable to value methodological diversity in assessment and analysis. Any potential source of information—qualitative and quantitative methods, laboratory and field measurements—offers potentially valuable data that can help clinicians better understand their clients.

BASIC TASKS

Building on previous work in combining science and practice in the helping professions (Hayes, Barlow, & Nelson-Gray, 1999; Maloney & Ward, 1976; Pepinsky & Pepinksy, 1954; Stricker & Trierweiler, 1995), in the remainder of this book I describe an approach to integrating conceptualization, assessment, analysis, and intervention in clinical work. In brief, the basic tasks with each client are to

1. Produce a tentative model of each client's process (i.e., problem causes) and outcome (i.e., effects) constructs;

2. Decide on methods to collect data on the elements of that model;

3. Analyze the collected data; and,

4. If necessary, modify the interventions, conceptualization, or assessments.

Chapters 2, 3, 4, and 5 describe these steps in detail.

This iterative process could (and often will) continue until termination, but practically stops when clinical work succeeds. The additional structure provides clinicians with feedback about key elements in the therapeutic process and thus enhances their ability to help clients.

⠶TWO⠶

CASE CONCEPTUALIZATION

———•◦•———

There is a universe of potentially available information about patients. One must decide what information is most relevant, how to obtain it, how to integrate what is obtained, and how to relate it to what are often nebulous and ill-defined categories. . . . One may have to understand precisely what is creating maladjustment, what client statements or behaviors actually mean, and whether and when client feedback is purposely or inadvertently misleading.

— Faust (1986, p. 423)

Our real choice is between using some sort of cognitive map drawn out of our training, reading, or other professional experiences, and wandering blindly through a maze of options, alternatives, and choices to which we respond randomly and ignorantly.

— Blocher (1987, p. 299)

Why is case conceptualization important? At the most basic level, conceptualization is important because it increases the potential for correctly identifying the causes and effects involved in clients' problems, which is what leads to effective interventions (Haynes, Spain, & Oliveira, 1993). Most clinicians are asked to help a pool of clients who present with a large number of different problems; the complexity of this client heterogeneity is often compounded for the clinician by a lack of knowledge, at least initially, about critical events in clients' lives (Garb, 1998; Kozak, 1996). Thus, clinicians face the difficult task of creating effective intervention plans using complex and incomplete information about each of the clients they are attempting to help. Given this context, clinical researchers (Layden et al., 1993; Needleman, 1999) have argued that case conceptualization can help clinicians organize and make sense of the overwhelming number of details present in any case; provide clinicians with an understanding of a client's unique processes and functioning sufficient to develop effective interventions; help clinicians predict client behaviors and responses to treatment; help clients understand their problems, reduce the seeming complexity of their problems, and, subsequently, increase their motivation for treatment; improve the working alliance as well as increase clients' confidence in the therapist, expectancies for change, and openness to methods derived from the conceptualization, particularly when clients see that their therapist has a sophisticated understanding of them.

Wiger (1999) summed up these benefits and more with a 22-word answer to the question of why clinicians should do case conceptualizations: "Accountability, clarity, communication, compensation, competency, compliance, consistency, dialogue, direction, documentation, ethics, evaluation, focus, goals, integration, measurement, objectives, planning, standardization, strengths, symptoms, validation" (p. 97).

WHAT INFORMATION IS NEEDED?

While clinical researchers have proposed a variety of definitions of case conceptualization (e.g., Beck, Emery, & Greenberg, 1995; Berman, 1997; Eells, 1997; Persons, 1989), they have also described a large number of potential elements that could be included in a case conceptualization (see Table 2.1).

Lambert (1994) and Mash and Hunsley (1993) endeavored to reduce this pool of elements to more fundamental categories, including (a) *symptoms* (e.g., clients' sleep difficulties, anger outbursts), (b) *functioning* (e.g., clients' work absences), (c) *domains* (e.g., clients' cognitive, affective, behavioral, interpersonal, and environmental problems), (d) *strengths* (e.g., clients' social supports, high self-efficacy in domains related to the presenting problem), and (e) *time* (e.g., intermediate versus long-term outcomes of therapy).

Table 2.1   Information Needed for Case Conceptualization

Source	Category
Needleman (1999)	1. The client's cognitive, affective, and behavioral responses to triggering events 2. The beliefs that determine those responses 3. The circumstances that initiate the client's maladaptive responses 4. The environment's responses to the client's behavior 5. The negative precipitants of the client's behavior 6. The learning history that contributes to the client's vulnerability
Berman (1997)	1. How age-appropriate is the client's behavior—physically, cognitively, and socially? 2. How might the client's abilities and values affect the treatment? 3. What role do peers, caregivers, and adults have for this person? 4. How might the client's sexual orientation, gender, or cultural background affect the treatment? 5. What is the client's medical history, religion, SES (socioeconomic status), education, history of physical and/or sexual abuse?
Prochaska (1995)	1. Client symptoms and situational problems 2. Maladaptive cognitions 3. Current interpersonal conflicts 4. Family and systems conflicts 5. Intrapersonal conflicts
Hill (1991)	1. Client variables (i.e., presenting problems, severity and chronicity of disturbance, personality characteristics, physical characteristics, educational background, intellectual abilities, expectations for counseling, motivation) 2. Counselor variables (i.e., type of training, intellectual abilities, expectations for counseling) 3. Setting variables (e.g., amount of fee, physical arrangement of room)
Lazarus (1997)	1. Behavior (e.g., What are the client's activities?) 2. Affect (e.g., How emotional is the client?) 3. Sensation (e.g., Is the client tuned in to bodily sensations?) 4. Imagery (e.g., Does the client have a vivid imagination?) 5. Cognition (e.g., Does the client like to analyze?) 6. Interpersonal relationships (e.g., How important are social interactions to the client?) 7. Drugs and/or biology (e.g., To what degree is the client health conscious?)

To simplify matters, *case conceptualization* in this text refers to a description of the linkages between process and outcome elements with a particular client. *Process* refers to causes, that is, the factors influencing client problems. The use of the term *cause* here is closer in meaning to what behaviorists have termed *functional relationships*, the only condition of which is that two variables share variance on any parameter (Haynes et al., 1993). This can be contrasted with more formal definitions of causal relationships where to be considered causal, two variables must covary, the causal variable must precede the effect, a logical mechanism exists to explain the causal relationship, and alternate explanations can be reasonably excluded (Haynes et al., 1993). Complementarily, *outcomes* refers to effects, the problems that result from the causative processes. Desired outcomes are clinical *goals*, whereas *objectives* are intermediate steps necessary to meet those more ultimate goals (Jongsma & Peterson, 1995; Wiger, 1999). When a clinician creates an explicit representation of process and outcome elements for a particular individual, this is a client *model*.

SOURCES OF INFORMATION FOR CONCEPTUALIZATION

Once a clinician has an idea of what information is needed for a conceptualization, where can it be obtained? The focus of this section is on the persons, methods, and bodies of knowledge that are most likely to provide useful information for conceptualization purposes. These are *clients, psychotherapy theories, research findings, nomothetic tests and interviews,* and *personal experiences of the clinician.*

Clients

Particularly in an idiographic approach, the client will be the most obvious source of information for the conceptualization. The client typically describes one or more *target complaints*, a set of problems that will become the focus of efforts at psychotherapeutic change. When the client begins to describe these problems, however, it often becomes apparent that a large number of potential causative factors exist. How do we know which ones to pay attention to? Which elements are most important?

The intake interview usually provides some organization and structure that guides the search for answers to these questions (Needleman, 1999; Sommers-Flanagan & Sommers-Flanagan, 1999). For example, Beck, Rush, Shaw, and Emery (1979) suggested that the initial interview be employed to assess psychopathology, gauge the client's strengths, and formulate a set of interventions. Similarly, the intake interviewer can begin to assess (a) which of the client's problems may be more amenable to intervention, (b) problems of which the client is unaware or underestimating in importance, (c) the client's interpersonal style, (d) which significant others (e.g., family, caseworkers, clinical staff) should be consulted for additional information, and (e) the history and context that surround the presenting problems. In addition, if the interviewer knows the client's major problem or problems, intake and interview procedures designed to obtain specific information about the problem or problems may be available. O'Donohue and Elliott (1991), for example, describe a procedure for obtaining specific information about sexual abuse with a child.

Psychotherapy Theories

A *theory* is a set of systematically related ideas intended to be applicable in a variety of conditions. A useful theory is like a map of a partially explored territory:

> The way theories make a difference in the world is thus not that they answer questions but that they guide and stimulate intelligent search. . . . One use of a theory, then, is that it prepares the conceptual categories within which the theoretician and the practitioner will ask . . . questions and design . . . experiments. (Weizenbaum, 1976, p. 152)

With a theory in mind, we can begin to apply it in an individual case. That is, we can create a model. Models employ different types of representations (e.g., physical, graphical) of the elements of a theory. We can build static and dynamic models: A *static model* represents some real-world phenomena at a single point in time; it does not change. A *dynamic model*, however, is a simulation of persons and events that change over time. A model can be said to satisfy a theory, that is, to some extent it operationalizes the rules of the theory (Weizenbaum, 1976). Moreover, models (and theories) are always simplifications of the phenomena they are intended to represent and thus will not behave exactly as the real-world phenomena do (Weizenbaum, 1976).

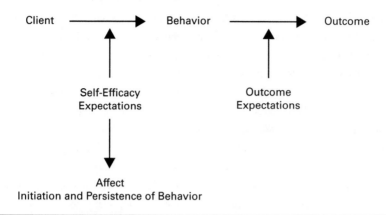

Figure 2.1   Efficacy and Outcome Expectations

SOURCE: "Self-Efficacy: Toward a Unifying Theory of Behavioral Change," by A. Bandura, 1977, *Psychological Review, 84*, pp. 191-215. Copyright©1977 by the American Psychological Association. Adapted with permission.

NOTE: Bandura proposed that individuals' expectancies about their ability to perform behaviors linked to desired outcomes strongly influenced their initiation and persistence of those behaviors. Those expectancies also influence what affect individuals experience.

A Sample of Individual Psychotherapy Theories

Psychotherapy theorists are typically concerned with understanding the processes involved in successful psychotherapy. Theorists have been quite prolific in their work, with some estimates placing the number of different counseling approaches (such as psychoanalytic, behavioral, and rational emotive) at over 400 (Karasu, 1986). More recently, attention has also been focused on a *common factors* approach to psychotherapy, in which a frequently occurring set of conditions (e.g., a helping relationship, client expectations of improvement) is believed to be operating across overtly different theories and therapeutic techniques (Frank & Frank, 1991; Wampold, 2001).

All psychotherapy theories identify potentially important domains for conceptualization (e.g., Bergin & Garfield, 1994; Corey, 1996; Corsini & Wedding, 1995). For example, Bandura (1977), as shown in Figure 2.1, proposed self-efficacy theory as a universal explanation for behavior change in psychotherapy.

Self-efficacy expectations refer to beliefs clients hold about whether they can perform specific behaviors. *Outcome expectations*, on the other hand, refer to beliefs about what outcomes will be produced by the performance of those specific behaviors. For example, students may know that if they study every night for 2 weeks before a major test, they will receive a high grade. However, many students may not believe that they can study that consistently and consequently do not attempt the task. Considerable research evidence (Bandura, 1977, 1986, 1997) supports the hypotheses that efficacy expectations strongly determine (a) what actions individuals will initiate and persist in and (b) the types of affect individuals will feel around certain tasks. For example, students with low self-efficacy for studying behaviors will feel anxious about studying. Bandura (1977) intended this theory to be applicable to all clients and all problems and proposed a set of interventions (e.g., modeling, direct performance of behaviors) specifically selected to improve self-efficacy.

Some psychotherapy theories focus on clients with common characteristics. Teyber (2000), for example, presents a therapeutic approach, applicable primarily to young adults, derived from interpersonal process theory, object relations theory, attachment theory, and family systems theory. Clinical work concentrates on *interpersonal problems*, assumes that the client's *family experiences* were the most important sources of learning, and relies on the *therapist-client relationship* to resolve problems. Much of the clinical process involves having clients verbally explore and reexperience the affect (particularly pain) surrounding their past family and social experiences, a therapeutic task younger children and adolescents may have difficulty performing. Also, Beutler and Harwood (2000) described how such client dimensions and personality characteristics as *impairment*, *distress*, *resistance*, and *coping style* can interact with interventions to influence therapeutic outcomes. *Coping style*, for example, refers to individuals' repetitive behaviors in interpersonal relationships that occur during times of stress and vulnerability; in other words, individuals' "ritualistic ways of coping with unwanted experiences" (Beutler & Harwood, 2000, p. 75). Beutler and Harwood maintain that individuals possess coping styles that can be characterized along an internal-external dimension where with regard to distressing experiences the focus is either on personal responsibility (as it is with internalizers) or on some other's responsibility (as it is with externalizers). Beutler and Harwood suggest that one of the tasks of effective therapy is to expose clients to avoided experiences.

Many students and clinicians will also be aware of therapeutic approaches designed for women and for persons of color (Neville & Mobley, 2001; Sue, Ivey, & Pedersen, 1996). Critics of traditional psychotherapy theories maintain that they apply mainly to White, middle-class men. Important factors such as sexism, racism, and other experiences related to ethnicity and gender have often been ignored in most psychotherapy theories. Women are more likely than men to present with problems related to childhood sexual abuse, sexual harassment, violence and rape, pregnancy and abortion, and eating disorders (Meier & Davis, 2001). Clinicians who employ feminist therapy focus on interventions that include consciousness raising, social and gender role analysis, and social activism (Israeili & Santor, 2000). Counselor prejudice and lack of bilingual clinicians have been proposed as reasons for the inadequacies of mental health services received by minority groups (Patterson, 1996).

Other theories posit common *stages of change* in therapy; these are sequences of events that most clients experience on their way to successful outcomes. For example, Prochaska and DiClemente (1983) described a trans-theoretical approach applicable to health behavior and mental health problems (Norcross & Goldfried, 1992; Velicer, Rossi, Prochaska, & DiClemente, 1996). Prochaska (1995) indicated that three fundamental dimensions of change can be described: *processes*, *stages*, and *levels*. The stages concept emphasizes that (a) change occurs over time and (b) problems can be characterized as a mixture of psychological traits and states. That is, client problems tend to be relatively stable, yet they are open to change with special interventions or effort.

Prochaska (1995) described change as unfolding over 6 stages:

Precontemplation is the stage when a person has no intention of changing the problem. In this stage other persons may be more aware of the problem than is the potential client. Persons who appear for therapy in this stage may feel coerced by others to seek help they do not believe they need. Research suggests that persons in this group are at highest risk for dropping out of therapy.

Contemplation is when a person knows a problem exists and she or he is thinking seriously about steps to remedy the problem. For example, smokers can be very aware of their need to stop yet remain in this contemplation stage for years (DiClemente & Prochaska, 1985).

Preparation is when a person intends to change and makes preliminary steps to do so. Smokers, for example, might smoke five fewer cigarettes a day in preparation for abstaining altogether.

Action is when individuals modify their behavior or environment to remedy the problem. Although many people see this stage as the whole of change, Prochaska (1995) emphasized that change includes the prerequisites to action and the effort to maintain changes following action.

Maintenance is when a person works to prevent relapse and fortify the changes made. Prochaska (1995) notes that this stage is an active one that typically lasts from 6 months to an indeterminate time past the initial action.

Termination is the stage when an individual is totally confident that the problem is solved across all previous problem situations. As Prochaska (1995) described it, "these people are no longer recovering—they are recovered" (p. 412).

Prochaska (1995) indicated that part of the importance of the stage theory is that different interventions can be more effective in certain stages. For example, consciousness raising can help clients become more aware of problems they are unaware they possess. Thus, case conceptualization and assessment of the client's stage of change are critical to selecting an intervention and enhancing the likelihood of successful outcome.

A Sample of Group Psychotherapy Theories

Yalom (1995) developed a useful set of explanations regarding the operation of successful outpatient group psychotherapy. Yalom believes that curative factors in effective groups result in the reduction of interpersonal and intrapsychic problems. Table 2.2 displays these factors and briefly describes them.

Although Yalom (1995) suggested that all of these factors are important, he also indicated that *cohesiveness* may be the most central factor in successful groups. In addition, Yalom noted that many of the factors are interdependent and may exert different levels of influence in different psychotherapy groups.

Table 2.2   Yalom's Curative Factors for Group Psychotherapy

Factor	Brief Description
Cohesiveness	Group members' ability to function together, their closeness, and the group's appeal to members
Installation of Hope	Group members' increasing their expectations for personal change, improvement
Universality	Members becoming aware that others in the group share similar problems
Providing Information	Members learning about mental health and similar issues through instruction and advice
Altruism	Group members learning how to give to others
Corrective Family	Group's resembling a family that accepts and supports its members
Experience	Members developing basic skills such as giving and listening to feedback, nonverbals
Social Skills Modeling	More advanced members evidencing skills that other members can imitate and try out
Existential Factors	Members' personal responsibility, feedback from others
Catharsis	Members' emotional expression leading to release of tension

While Yalom's approach tends to focus on potentially important process elements in group psychotherapy, other theories suggest a set of conditions or sequences of actions that should be observed in effective groups. For example, one of the central concerns in conducting therapeutic groups is determining how *structured* they should be (Kaul & Bednar, 1994). That is, to what extent should the leader direct the group and set tasks for them to perform? Some group theorists emphasize the beneficial effect of greater structure, believing that it reduces ambiguity in the group, decreases subsequent anxiety, and allows more productive social interactions (Kaul & Bednar, 1994). In some groups, however, leaders may leave the group unstructured so that they may observe how individuals respond to the resulting ambiguity and anxiety. Such responses in group are assumed to be illustrative of how individuals respond to similar situations outside the group.

In highly structured groups, leaders may look for opportunities to relax the degree of structure so that more interpersonal, *emotion-focused tasks* can occur (Kaul & Bednar, 1994). Even the most emotionally restricted individuals will occasionally step outside the group structure. That is, group clients will attempt to connect emotionally and interpersonally in ways unplanned by the leader. For example, in an initial session group members may be responding to a leader request to state their purpose for being in the group. If one member responds to another's statement, perhaps with support or feedback, the group leader might allow the interaction between them to continue for a few minutes, even if the group task is delayed. In addition, some research indicates that reducing external *feedback* during practice may enhance the strength of learned skills (Kaul & Bednar, 1994). This suggests that once group members have mastered a skill, leaders may reduce their reinforcement and feedback of that behavior. In general, group leaders tend to reduce structure in their groups as the group increases its cohesiveness and self-directedness.

Research Findings

Clinical outcome and process research can also suggest conceptualization constructs that enjoy at least some degree of empirical support. Because some evidence indicates that clients prefer treatment decisions that are at least partially based on research evidence (O'Donohue, Fisher, Plaud, & Link, 1989), explicitly using research-based information may lend credibility to clincans' treatment planning.

Researchers have identified causal factors for problems such as depression, eating disorders, conduct disorders, and adolescent aggression (Haynes et al., 1993). Also, Orlinksy, Grawe, and Parks's (1994) review of research results found that positive outcomes in individual psychotherapy were associated with such process constructs as *the amount clients talk*, proper handling of *termination*, strength of the *therapeutic bond*, and *timeliness in starting treatment*. Hill (1991) identified key process elements such as *ancillary behaviors* (e.g., nonverbal behaviors), *verbal behaviors, covert behaviors* (e.g., therapist intentions), *therapeutic content* (e.g., content analysis of dreams), *strategies* (e.g., analysis of transference), *interpersonal manner* (e.g., therapist empathy), and *therapeutic relationship* (e.g., working alliance). Bednar and Kaul's (1994) review of research in group psychotherapy found that *cohesion, interpersonal learning, catharsis*, and *self-understanding* were important factors for some groups and types of clients.

Basic research (as contrasted with applied research) may also be a useful source of information for case conceptualizations (see Lipsey, 1990). For example, social psychological research may provide information applicable to group work about *norms* (i.e., how a person should act and feel in a group), *goals* (what is desirable for a group and its members to achieve), and *values* (what is desirable for a group to be and become) (Mills, 1984). More recently, Strong and colleagues (Strong, 1995; Strong, Welsh, Corcoran, & Hoyt, 1992) described how social influence theory can be employed to describe important interpersonal processes in individual clinical situations. Based on a review and extrapolation of research on interpersonal behavior and constructs such as *relationship dependence*, *dominance*, and *affiliation*, Strong and colleagues indicate that (a) the degree of a clients' dependence on the clinician affects their responsiveness to therapy, (b) new ideas introduced by clinicians stimulate change in clients, and (c) successful clinical relationships generate a psychological convergence over time between clinicians and clients.

Finally, case studies represent an important source of information about case conceptualization for many clinicians. Although case studies lack the rigor of other research methods (Heppner, Kivlighan, & Wampold, 1999; Kazdin, 1980), they provide considerable detail both about a specific client or problem type (e.g., important context such as history, family background, and other contributing factors) and a particular approach to intervention that the clinician can generalize to cases in her or his practice (Hoshmand, 1994). Also, case narratives are usually easy to understand and remember, characteristics often not associated with other research methodologies. The particulars of the reported case, however, may not generalize to other clients.

Nomothetic Tests and Interviews

Although there is disagreement about their usefulness in promoting treatment success (Hayes et al., 1987), nomothetic tests and interviews represent another potential source of clinically relevant information. For example, Graham (1990) wrote that "the MMPI-2 [Minnesota Multiphasic Personality Inventory-2] should be used solely to generate hypotheses or inferences about an examinee" (p. 200), noting that the test can provide information relevant to etiology, symptoms, interpersonal relationships, diagnosis, and psycho-pathology. Graham (1990; see also Butcher, 1990; Maruish, 1994) indicated that the MMPI and tests such as the Symptom

Checklist-Revised (SCL-90-R), Beck Depression Inventory-2 (BDI-2), and State-Trait Anxiety Inventory (STAI) can provide information relevant to the choice of intervention and the client's response to different interventions. For example, test scores that indicate that a client is very defensive suggest that she or he is not a good candidate for psychotherapy; on the other hand, a high Ego Strength score on the MMPI-2 indicates that the person is likely to be receptive to therapy.

Clinician Experiences

While experienced clinicians have developed a well of professional knowledge from which to draw, novice clinicians often formulate their client conceptualizations on the basis of their personal experiences (Beutler, 2000; Meier, 1999). That is, students tend to extrapolate explanations and solutions from their life experiences to the client's situations. This may or may not be useful, as there exists an enormous variety of experiences among therapists as well as considerable variability between the fit of students' experiences and those of the current client. In general, students should be very cautious when they apply their personal experiences to clients and not assume that clients experience the world as they do (see Meier & Davis, 2001; Trierweiler & Stricker, 1998). A tension often exists for instructors between encouraging students to develop the self as a clinical instrument and helping students remain sufficiently detached so as not to confuse the client's experiences with their own.

CREATING A CASE CONCEPTUALIZATION

Once a clinician has gathered information relevant to a particular client, how should she or he proceed to create a case conceptualization? As shown in Table 2.3, clinical researchers have suggested a variety of approaches.

These recommendations vary in complexity, and they either implicitly or explicitly include the content of case conceptualization. These procedures include such disparate elements as (a) the application of general psychotherapy theories to particular clients (e.g., Berman, 1997; Murdock, 1991); (b) methods for minimizing errors in clinical judgment (Biggs, 1988; Hanna,

Table 2.3   Approaches to Case Conceptualization

Source	*Description*
Berman (1997)	1. Select a theoretical orientation appropriate to client. 2. Use a premise and supporting material as key features in the concept. 3. Use long- and short-term goals for the treatment plan. 4. Develop an effective personal writing style.
Biggs (1988)	Utilize a case presentation model designed to enhance divergent and relativistic reasoning.
Borders et al. (1994)	Consider the client a case study, collecting and analyzing counseling process data.
Cummings et al. (1990)	1. After each session, consider the most important client responses; 2. Arrange the responses on a large sheet of paper, showing how different concepts are related; 3. Draw lines between the concepts that are closely related; 4. Draw a circle around any cluster of concepts that belong together, labeling each.
Hanna et al. (1996)	Use dialectical thinking (i.e., view constructs as having two poles).
Murdock (1991)	Apply counseling theory to a particular client using a set of described procedures.
Neufeldt et al. (1995)	Gather information (including cultural and SES data), set a problem, and develop a change strategy.
Neufeldt et al. (1996)	Learn to tolerate ambiguity and accept not knowing, to consider theory and personal experiences, and to understand personal biases.
Needleman (1999)	1. Obtain identifying information, the presenting problem, and information on precipitants (e.g., clients' current situations, major problems, and precipitating events). 2. Create an exhaustive list of problems, issues, and therapy-relevant behaviors to help remind clients about the problems that need to be addressed. 3. Learn the relevant client beliefs (i.e., schemas that individuals use to perceive and remember information). 4. Identify the origins of clients' core beliefs (which is helpful for designing interventions). 5. Identify clients' vicious cycles and/or maintaining factors, focusing on those that are to be interrupted.

Table 2.3 *(Continued)*

Source	Description
	6. List treatment goals, list potential obstacles to treatment, and create a treatment plan (focusing on realistic goals for the most important problems) that are agreeable to therapist and client.
Nelson & Neufeldt (1998)	Use a constructivist approach: Create working hypotheses that are reformulated over time; develop into a reflective practitioner.
Schwitzer (1996)	Use an inverted pyramid model to perform stepwise clinical decision making.
Wantz & Morran (1994)	Use a divergent hypothesis formation strategy.

Glordano, & Bemak, 1996; Wantz & Morran, 1994); (c) the collection and analysis of data relevant to the conceptualization and related hypotheses (Borders, Bloss, Cashwell, & Rainey, 1994; Nelson & Neufeldt, 1998); (d) encouraging the clinician to focus on her or his experiences with the client as a source of information (Neufeldt, Karno, & Nelson, 1996); and (e) representing the conceptualization graphically (Cummings, Hallberg, Martin, Slemon, & Heibert, 1990). More detailed descriptions of procedures for creating conceptualizations can be found in Gottman and Leiblum (1974; see their Figure 1, Flow Chart of Psychotherapy) and in Orlinsky and colleagues (1994; see Figure 8.1, Generic Model of Psychotherapy).

The core of these recommendations is incorporated below in seven steps for creating a case conceptualization:

Identify the initial process and outcome elements.

Learn the etiology of client problems.

Choose interventions for selected problems.

Consider the time frame of interventions and outcomes.

Represent the conceptualization explicitly.

Include at least one alternative explanation.

Consider the model's balance between parsimony and comprehensiveness.

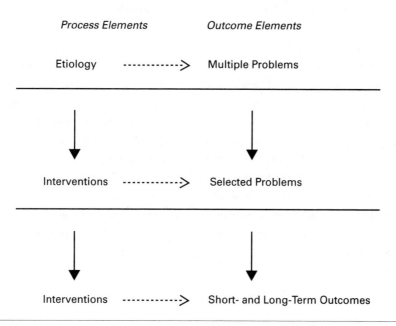

Figure 2.2   The Three Levels of a Case Conceptualization

Seven Steps for Creating a Case Conceptualization

Identify the Initial Process and Outcome Elements

The first step in the development of any case conceptualization is to select the important process and outcome elements based on the client's presenting problems. As described above, the central purpose of the initial intake inter-view is to identify one or more key problems identified by the client. As shown in Figure 2.2, we can describe these client problems in terms of processes that lead to a set of outcomes. We can think of client processes in terms of the causes of client problems and the outcomes as the effects or results of the causative processes. Process and outcome elements themselves can be further elaborated in terms of three levels: (a) exploring the *etiology* of the client's presenting problem, which usually leads to the identification of *multiple problems;* (b) choosing from among *multiple problems* the *selected problems* that become the focus of therapeutic *interventions*; and (c) intervening with those selected problems, which will produce *short-term* and *long-term* *outcomes*.

Figure 2.2 illustrates the three levels at which case conceptualization encompasses process and outcome elements. *Process elements* refer to causative factors that influence effects or outcomes in clients. *Causes* can be described at the level of etiology (i.e., the precipitants and maintaining influences) and at the level of interventions (i.e., the actions aimed at resolving selected outcomes). *Outcome elements* include all of the multiple problems brought by the client to counseling. Of that initial group of problems, conceptualization focuses on those problems selected for intervention. The selected problems can be considered in terms of interventions intended to influence short-term or intermediate outcomes as well as long-term outcomes that will be addressed or affected after successful completion of the intermediate steps.

Learn the Etiology of Client Problems

At the first level, *etiological hypotheses* refer to "the causes, precipitants, and maintaining influences of a person's psychological, interpersonal, and behavior problems" (Eells, 1997, p. 1). The etiology depends on the particular theory we employ to interpret the client's reports and explanations about causes. A psychoanalytic therapist would see a phobic client as avoiding the feared object in order to defend an unconscious wish. A behavioral clinician would assume that one or more learning experiences (i.e., the antecedents and consequences of behavior with the phobic object) led to the development of the phobia. A cognitive therapist would focus on how the client perceives and thinks about the phobic object, particularly how that thinking might be irrational or biased. Although an understanding of the etiology of a client's problems may not always be necessary for a resolution of those problems, such understanding should increase the clinician's probability of selecting useful interventions.

It is important to reemphasize the benefits and importance of considering psychotherapy and other theories as sources of etiological information, because clinicians, particularly student clinicians, may simply ignore it (Meier, 1999). Students often create conceptualizations based on their personal experiences (when trying to explain etiology) or on simple imitation of the therapeutic

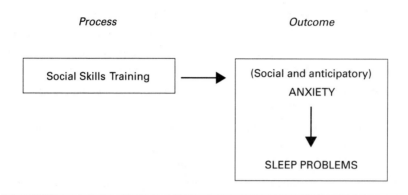

Figure 2.3   Therapeutic Technique as Simplistic Process Element

techniques they have observed others employ (when trying to propose inter-ventions). As shown in Figure 2.3, a student may create a model where process is simply described as a therapeutic technique.

Two difficulties exist with simply inserting a therapeutic technique— without understanding the etiological foundations of the client's problem— into the process component of a client model. First, if the technique does not work, you have little basis for knowing what to try next. If a student group leader simply tried to create cathartic experiences for group members, for example, knowledge of when and why to implement that approach would be important. If the cathartic technique was not helpful, it would be important to know the remaining curative factors described by Yalom (1995). Second, focusing exclusively on technique may prevent the clinician from thinking deeply about clients and observing potentially important therapeutic processes as they occur. In contrast, creating a client model at least partially on the basis of relevant theory and research means that the student is learning and applying a deeper knowledge base. Although some clinical educators believe in helping students learn how to use the self as a clinical instrument, few instructors would recommend ignoring the theoretical and research liter-atures, whatever their flaws (Peterson, 1992). In addition, clinicians may bring issues, such as *countertransference* for particular clients and *cultural centrism,* that distort their ability to perceive clients' processes and outcomes (MacDonald, 1996).

Choose Interventions for Selected Problems

As Figure 2.2 illustrates, from the level of etiological process can flow at least some of the clinician's ideas about the second layer of the conceptualization, *interventions*. In essence, this step folds the *treatment plan* into the conceptualization, thereby increasing the chances that etiology is at least considered when clinicians plan interventions. Eells (1997) noted that ideas about intervention can include the type, frequency, and duration of interventions directed toward clinical goals. At this level outcomes are also considered, in terms of *multiple* and *selected problems*. Although an intake interview should be as thorough as possible to learn about client problem areas, a case conceptualization need not include all the problems that a client brings to therapy. Some clients bring only one or two clearly defined problems, although most cases involve multiple or poorly defined problems. The task is to select a smaller subset of problems that become the focus of conceptualization.

Criteria for selection into the smaller problem group include outcomes with causes that (a) are more amenable to influence in therapy or are prerequisites to modifying other behaviors (Haynes et al., 1993); (b) are of greater importance to the client or significant others (Hartman, 1984); (c) are most likely to be modifiable within the session or time limits of the client, agency, or insurer; and (d) involve activities that are dangerous, socially repugnant, depart from normal functioning, or significantly interfere with client functioning (Hartman, 1984).

While these selection criteria focus on client processes and outcomes, the therapist's theoretical orientation represents another significant influence on selection of target problems (Cone, 2001). For example, suppose a female client comes to therapy and reports that she would like to lose 15 pounds before her wedding in 6 months. A behavior therapist might take "weight loss" as the major outcome at face value, whereas a feminist therapist might focus on eating disorders and societal values about women's appearances. Any therapist with knowledge of the research on weight loss might want to discuss the difficulty of maintaining an initial weight loss. In any event, some balance must be struck between what the client brings to therapy and the therapist's orientation.

In general, the most useful sources of information for creating an initial conceptualization are theory and research related to the selected outcome and process elements. If an empirically supported intervention is known to influence the client's major outcome, for example, it makes sense to insert that intervention into the client model and employ it with the client. Modification of the model and subsequent treatment decisions occur when client-specific data show that it is necessary or advisable to do so.

Consider the Time Frame of Interventions and Outcomes

The third level of the case conceptualization focuses on identifying *short-term, intermediate,* and *long-term outcomes* (Berman, 1997; Needleman, 1999). These terms refer to a chain of events or processes that must occur before a desired long-term outcome is achieved. Similarly, Hill (1991) differentiated among *immediate outcomes* (which occur right after a therapeutic intervention within a session), outcomes of a counseling event (which occur after a series of therapeutic interventions), *session outcomes* (which occur after one specific session), and the *treatment outcome* (which is the final or ultimate outcome).

Problem resolution can be considered a series of steps that must be taken before a more ultimate goal is accomplished. A behavioral perspective on phobia, for example, would suggest that a client should experience exposure to the phobic object in a series of graduated steps before fear of the object is reduced or extinguished. From any therapeutic perspective, however, a set of in-session interventions leads to impacts on the client both within the session and immediately postsession (see, e.g., Stiles, 1980). The client may further apply those experiences in subsequent life situations, leading to further learning and movement toward a new set of issues to be discussed and experienced during the next therapy session. Intermediate constructs shown by research to be predictive of treatment success for individual clients and families include therapeutic alliance, client satisfaction with therapy, and the degree of client involvement in treatment planning (Bickman et al., 2000).

Failure to recognize intermediate steps can result in case conceptualizations where the linkage between process and outcome elements is too distant and the subsequent interventions ineffective. As shown in Figure 2.4, a clinician who provides only support and empathy to a student with failing grades—who also needs better study skills, a quiet place and time to do homework, stable family relationships, and increased motivation—is unlikely to see the student achieve significantly better grades. This is not to say that the initial process is unimportant; clinician empathy may provide the relationship foundation that encourages the client to learn study skills and explore

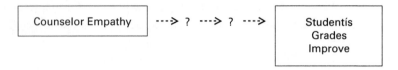

Figure 2.4   What Are the Missing Links in the Process-Outcome Chain?

Figure 2.5   A Basic Process-Outcome Model

motivation about school. Client models, however, may contain constructs that are connected distally, with unspecified moderators between the proposed process and outcome factors. If treatment is failing, consider whether the conceptualization (and subsequent intervention) could be improved by considering additional intermediate process and outcome constructs.

Short-term and long-term outcomes may also be related to chronological events in the client's life. A college student who is about to return home during a break in the academic year may be about to face a temporary set of family stressors largely unrelated to the presenting, long-term problem of uncertainty about career choice. And, as discussed below, elaboration of short-term and long-term goals is particularly critical in the case of treatment failure. When progress is not being made, a particularly useful step is to consider whether treatment goals are too ambitious and could be improved by specifying more short-term approximations (Berman, 1997).

Also note that in the context of discussing short-term, intermediate, and long-term outcomes, the distinctions between process and outcome constructs are arbitrary. Suppose, for example, a client presents with a sleep problem that is affecting work performance. This issue is represented in Figure 2.5.

In this illustration, we can designate sleep problems as the process construct and poor work performance as the outcome of interest. However, if we introduce moderators between these two elements (Hanley, 2001), the picture becomes more complex, as shown in Figure 2.6.

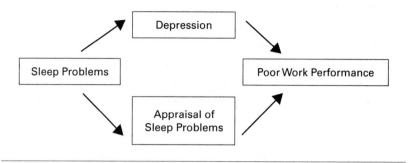

Figure 2.6   The Moderators of Factors Influencing Poor Work Performance

Which element is designated as a process construct and which is designated as outcome is arbitrary, depending on the sequence of the model. The model in Figure 2.6 is partially based on one proposed by Hanley (2001).

In this model, sleep problems cause depression, which in turn negatively influences work performance; the client's perceptions of the sleep problems also hinder work performance. The choice of which constructs to designate as process or outcome factors, however, is arbitrary. For example, sleep problems may be considered as the initial process that caused the intermediate problem of depression, which caused the long-term decrement in work performance. Sleep problems also could be considered another process factor that influences work performance. In summary, the designation of factors as process or outcomes is less important than creating models that help the clinician to understand the client and devise useful interventions.

Represent the Conceptualization Explicitly

Once these three levels of the conceptualization have been considered for a particular client, the next step is to represent the conceptualization. Note that we can apply theories to clients explicitly (e.g., drawing out behavioral or psychodynamic explanations that fit a particular client) or implicitly (e.g., applying our personal schemas and belief systems to the client with little or no awareness). Regardless of the source or type, it is valuable to make theory explicit in conceptualization. The more explicit the conceptualization, the more likely it is that we can test, modify, and act on it (see Berman, 1997; Loesch, 1977; Needleman, 1999). An explicit model illustrates the relations of components more clearly than does an implicit model and clarifies theoretical weaknesses and implications (Creswell, 1994; Duncan, 1985). Another important purpose of using an explicit model is that it helps the clinician know what to pay attention to and what to ignore in the rich and complex information communicated between client and clinician (Kozak, 1996).

Three methods used to make a conceptualization explicit are to (a) represent it graphically, (b) write a concise summary, or (c) explain it thoroughly to a supervisor or colleague. The method employed here, called *graphic modeling* (see Chmielewski & Dansereau, 1998; Mattaini, 1993; Pitre, Dansereau, Newbern, & Simpson, 1998), possesses many advantages. For example, graphic models can provide the big picture of client processes and outcomes by focusing attention on important elements *and* maintaining awareness of the comprehensive clinical situation:

1. models can help clinicians plan and implement helpful interventions;

2. models can also help clinicians keep track of evolving relations among process and outcome elements (Maxwell, 1996);

3. models enhance our recall of client information (Chmielewski & Dansereau, 1998; Czuchry & Dansereau, 1998);

4. models can help clinicians summarize the substance and sequence of client information (see Tufte, 1983, 1990);

5. models enhance communicability of the case conceptualization with clients, supervisors, and others who need to understand client dynamics;

6. and, according to some evidence, models can improve treatment outcomes (Pitre et al., 1998).

Learning to represent client process and outcomes with a graphic model can be a difficult task initially. Although most student clinicians can verbalize some process and outcome elements about their clients, these are often presented in the form of simple lists. The task of moving from a list to a graphic representation of relations between process and outcome forces the clinician to perform the more difficult task of organizing important elements. Supervised practice is particularly important with this task. Although graphic models are the preferred format here, the information in the conceptualization may need to be formatted for the particular clinical setting. The Joint Commission on Accreditation of Healthcare Organizations (JCAHO) standards, for example, require that a time frame be specified for each objective in a treatment plan and that specific criteria be set for discharge (JCAHO, 1997). The type of content in the model may also be predetermined; clinicians may have to include *symptoms* in treatment plans where medical necessity is the standard by which treatment is authorized (Wiger, 1999).

Include at Least One Alternative Explanation

Alternative explanations are process-outcome links other than the major relationships initially proposed in the case conceptualization. If you suggest, for example, that a client's depression is caused by irrational beliefs (Persons, 1989), what other potential causes might account for the depression?

Alternative explanations are worth considering, from the beginning to the end of therapy, with every case conceptualization. As discussed further in Chapter 5, the basic concern is that everyone is susceptible to the Hypothesis Confirmation Bias (HCB), the tendency to crystallize on an initial hypothesis and then ignore later disconfirming information. The obvious antidote is to create and keep in mind alternative explanations to the initial working hypotheses (Platt, 1977). That is, what other ideas might explain this client's processes and outcomes? Different psychotherapy theories offer obvious sources of alternative conceptualizations. Through data provided via formal and informal clinical assessment (as described in Chapters 3 and 4), the client and the clinical process provide feedback about the usefulness of the conceptualization.

Alternative explanations are likely to become more apparent as therapy progresses. Initial case conceptualizations may change as the therapeutic alliance strengthens and clients deepen their exploration and description of the presenting problem (see Egan, 1998). In general, be open to revising your initial client model. Many client problems do not possess what Beutler and Hamblin (1986) termed *persistent relevance* (in which the key problems at the beginning of therapy remain the chief issues throughout the course of therapy). Although the client's target complaints are typically the initial focus of the case conceptualization, redefinition and clarification of client problems can and should occur throughout treatment (Battle et al., 1966; Mash & Hunsley, 1993; Ridley, Li, & Hill, 1998). Problem identification is often not straightforward and objective but a task that evolves as the clinician and client develop their relationship and together begin to identify meaning and significance in the client's experiences (Hill, 1982; Madill, Widdicombe, & Barkham, 2001). Acuff and colleagues (1999) noted that the

> primary issue for which the person sought treatment may not turn out to be the primary focus in therapy. External stressors may lead to a precipitous decline in the functioning of the patient, or the true nature of the problem may not be discernible until therapy has been underway for some time. The more knowledge clinicians accumulate about the causes and development of a client's problem—and the better the quality of that information—the greater the number of potential explanations and avenues for effective assessment and intervention. (p. 571)

With every conceptualization, during the course of the intervention, I recommend that you add at least one etiological process element, one intervention process element, and one outcome element that represent potential alternatives to the major initial process-outcome elements proposed in your client model. In other words, explicitly answer the questions:

1. What is another possible cause for the client's selected problem or problems?
2. What is another possible intervention for the problem or problems?
3. What might be another outcome worthy of further consideration?

Answers to these three basic questions can be added to the case conceptualization and represented graphically as well. And as described below in the section on treatment failure, there also may be instances in which a complete reconstruction of the case conceptualization is warranted.

Consider the Model's Balance
Between Parsimony and Comprehensiveness

This final step (see O'Neill, 1993; Persons, 1989) involves a simple question that requires thought: Does the client model identify the fewest number of beliefs and processes that comprehensively explain the client's problems?

Parsimony refers to whether the elements in a theory are as simple as possible, without being trivial or simplistic. Parsimony is important for three reasons. First, creating a model is inherently time consuming both in construction and implementation; keeping the model as simple as possible helps to minimize the amount of required time and effort. Second, the model is intended to be useful both out of session (as an organizer for treatment planning) and in session (when deciding how to proceed during a particular interaction with a client). One rule of thumb is that if the clinician can recall the client model during the session, it is not too complex. Third, researchers employ the principle of parsimony (i.e., Ockham's Razor; Vogt, 1999) when evaluating different theories: If all else is equal, prefer the simpler explanation. This is a useful guideline in clinical situations as well.

As noted above, students' first response to model construction is often to create long lists of process and outcome elements. Martin, Slemon, Hiebert, Hallberg, and Cummings (1989), for example, found that when conceptualizing specific client problems, experienced clinicians identify fewer constructs than novices do. Similarly, experienced clinicians appear to employ conceptualization constructs more consistently across sessions and across clients than novices do (Cummings et al., 1990). Although a tension exists between parsimony and comprehensiveness, it is almost always better for beginners initially to limit the number of elements in case conceptualizations and add them as necessary.

Knowledge of psychotherapy theories can also help in the construction of models that balance parsimony and completeness. Theory helps students turn lists of process and outcome elements into models by providing categories and relations among concepts that can help succinctly summarize the specifics of a particular client.

A CONCEPTUALIZATION EXAMPLE

Luke, a 25-year-old single, gay, White male, has few friends and his family of origin lives far away. He also has few financial resources, having moved to this city 6 months ago for a new job as a teacher. Luke reports that he has trouble falling asleep at night because he is worrying about what he perceives as the day's social mistakes as well as potentially troublesome social situations on the following day. He reports occasionally ruminating about interactions with others during the day at school, although the objects of his rumination are both fellow teachers and persons he knows outside of work. Most of Luke's ruminations concern his belief that others are paying special attention to him and expecting him to make mistakes in social interactions; thus, Luke closely monitors and evaluates how he is behaving and speaking with others, including his students.

Another factor influencing Luke's therapy is that it will be paid by insurance through Managed Care Company X. This company does not provide reimbursement for any psychological condition that it considers chronic and only authorizes sessions in blocks of 3. Although the insurer advertises that clients can receive up to 20 sessions per year, in reality only 6 to 9 sessions are authorized annually (see Davis & Meier, 2001). Given that Luke cannot afford to pay for additional sessions, 9 sessions is likely to be the total number of sessions available to him.

The first step in creating a conceptualization for Luke is to identify initial process and outcome elements. Two outcomes Luke wishes to change are sleep problems and social anxiety. Regarding process elements, Luke clearly has little social support and may have distorted cognitions around his social interactions.

The second step involves learning the etiology of Luke's problem. He reports a history of conflict with others about being shy and being gay. Although he has not come out to his family, his father has been very critical of gays and lesbians whenever Luke has brought up the topic. Only two of his close friends in the small town where he grew up know that he is gay, although other peers and adults who suspect this have ridiculed him. A quiet person, Luke tends not to initiate social interactions and spends a considerable amount of time by himself; his peers see him as a loner. Thus, Luke's history of conflict with his father and peers leads him to expect others to be critical of him.

Choosing potential interventions for selected problems is the third step in the case conceptualization. Given Luke's social history and presenting problems of sleep problems and social anxiety, a variety of possible interventions are apparent. One approach would be to address what you believe is the most salient issue for Luke, the sleep problems, and its most immediate antecedent, distorted cognitions, using some variety of cognitive therapy (e.g., Beck, 1976). This might also make sense in the context of the fourth step in conceptualization, consider the time frame, in that a managed care company is paying for treatment and Luke has no resources himself to extend therapy. Thus, a brief intervention that focuses on a short-term outcome would seem an appropriate starting point.

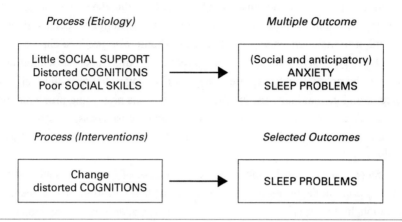

Figure 2.7 One Representation of the Process and Outcome Elements for Luke

Figure 2.8 An Alternative Explanation for Luke's Sleep Problems

Graphically the key elements of Luke's case may be represented as shown in Figure 2.7.

Other therapeutic schools might view this representation as incomplete (in terms of important concepts), misleading, or simply in need of additional information (e.g., whether Luke has lacked social support in the past or just during the current transition). As I created this model, I became aware that Luke's anticipatory anxiety would be a likely cause of his sleep problems as well as an outcome resulting from his lack of social support, distorted cognitions, and possible poor social skills. Thus, an alternative explanation for Luke's conceptualization (shown in Figure 2.8) is that the anticipatory anxiety should be the more immediate outcome of interest.

Other possible alternative explanations include the perspective of more affectively oriented therapists (e.g., Gestalt, Rogerian), who might devise interventions that focus directly on the experience of anxiety.

Relationship-oriented therapists might attend to the development of the therapeutic relationship, thus providing Luke with additional social support. Attention to the client-therapist relationship should also produce clues about how Luke typically interacts with and thinks about other people. In addition, it might be productive to explore in depth Luke's own thoughts and feelings about being gay and how this might be related to his presenting problems. In the interest of balancing parsimony and comprehensiveness, however, the current model (Figure 2.7) is about as complicated as I could recall and use in therapy.

Steps 1 through 7 described above in the case of Luke represent a good starting point in the development of his case conceptualization. The conceptualization, however, is just that: a starting point. The additional information that inevitably develops over the course of therapy often results in a modification of one or more of the conceptualization elements.

TREATMENT FAILURE

Case conceptualization requires the resources of clinicians' time and energy, which are often scarce. Thus, in some clinical settings it may be feasible to conduct thorough conceptualizations only in particular circumstances. One of those circumstances should be *treatment failure*, instances when clients fail to make progress in therapy (Beck, 1995; Clark, 1999; Leahy, 1999; Mash & Hunsley, 1993; Persons, 1989; Riskind & Williams, 1999; Tompkins, 1999). This can be a particularly difficult topic to address directly given its sensitive nature for both clinician and client.

Recall that Lambert and colleagues (2001) found that outcome scores were better for clients who initially were not making progress but whose therapist was receiving feedback than for clients who initially were not making progress and whose therapist received no feedback. The major impact of feedback on outcome appeared to be with clients evidencing an initial treatment failure; no differences at termination appeared between clients who were making progress throughout therapy and whose therapists were and were not receiving feedback. And although feedback to therapists was associated with improved scores for clients not making progress, 75% of this group was still classified as having no change or deteriorated at termination. Lambert and colleagues also noted that the main effect of feedback appeared to be that therapists

Table 2.4   Potential Indicators of Treatment Failure

Frequent telephone consults	Failure to complete homework
Failure to pay	Missed appointments
Silence	Evasion
Cutting off emotion	Rejecting assistance
Unreasonable client expectations	Intoxication
Refusal of treatment	Premature termination
Nonresponse or small response	Worsening of presenting symptoms
Failure of treatment effects to generalize over time or situations	

SOURCE: Blau (1988) and Mash and Hunsley (1993, pp. 292-301).

kept their failing clients in treatment longer and their steadily improving clients for fewer sessions.

Because of clients' heterogeneous responses to treatment, many cases are likely to evidence some signs of treatment success as well as treatment failure. Some potential signs of treatment failure described in the literature are listed in Table 2.4.

Any description or definition of treatment failure that specifies particular indicators, however, is likely to miss the idiographic nature of clinical work. A more useful orientation is to examine treatment failure in terms of a lack of positive gains or the continued presence of negative events on constructs of clinical relevance to particular individuals. A case conceptualization should be specific enough and include sufficient context to indicate when treatment is failing in a particular case. For example, treatment of a client with a history of frequent hospitalizations might be considered a failure unless the hospitalizations decrease in frequency. Once that goal was achieved, however, failure might be redefined in terms of goals such as holding a job or maintaining long-term relationships.

More surprising than the simple presence of treatment failure is evidence that many therapists do not reconsider their treatment plans in the face of such failure. Kendall, Kipnis, and Otto-Salaj (1992) noted that previous research suggests that many therapists believe that if they follow generally accepted procedures, success is inevitable. Kendall and colleagues also found that research indicates that when clients fail, therapists tend to rate themselves as the most important cause, followed by client characteristics such as ability to benefit from therapy. Consequently, Kendall and colleagues surveyed 315 psychotherapists to investigate the amount of treatment failure in their practice and their explanations for such failure. The results are as follows:

1. About 11% of each clinician's clients were not making progress.

2. The majority of therapists who planned to continue treating failing clients had no alternative treatment plans.

3. Their theoretical orientations influenced clinicians' judgments about the length of time necessary before they concluded that no progress was being made. Psychodynamic therapists averaged 14 months before reaching this conclusion, whereas cognitive-behavioral therapists averaged 6 months.

4. Despite the literature showing that the severity of clients' problems is a strong influence on lack of progress (e.g., Meier & Letsch, 2000), most clinicians failed to cite severity as a reason for failure. In fact, therapists' written comments indicated that they generally believed that no problem was too severe to be treated by psychotherapy. Kendall and colleagues (1992) concluded that "therapists failed to take into account the severity of their clients' symptoms when explaining both probable causes of their clients' lack of progress, and when evaluating their clients' functioning" (p. 278).

5. In contrast to previous research, therapists in this study rated clients' "inability to benefit from therapy" (p. 275) as the most important reason for their lack of progress. Therapists rated themselves as the least likely cause.

Other reasons may also account for therapists' relative inattention to treatment failure. First, defining treatment failure depends on the therapeutic approach used to interpret therapeutic events (Mash & Hunsley, 1993). An initial increase in symptoms, for example, may be seen as indicative of progress in paradoxical and behavioral approaches. Second, Kendall and colleagues (1992) noted that the literature on treatment failure is relatively sparse; thus, few guidelines exist about what to do when clients fail to make progress. Third, because objective criteria for defining progress or failure are often lacking, the amount of change will also depend upon the source's perspective (i.e., therapist, client, significant other) (Kendall et al., 1992). Kendall and colleagues (1992) concluded that a pressing need exists for therapists to consider alternative strategies when dealing with clients not making therapeutic progress.

Thorough reconceptualization of the client should be one of the first techniques attempted when treatment failure becomes apparent. In this regard, recent publications provide useful concepts to consider. Leahy (1999), for example, proposes a conflict between the therapist's desire for the client to maximize possible gains and the client's wish to reduce possible additional losses. In this view, the client has significant aversion to risk, very high criteria for defining gains, and the belief that loss is intolerable because it will set off further losses (Clark, 1999). From this perspective, the therapist should focus more on the client's anticipated losses and less on the possible gains. Riskind and Williams (1999) proposed a model specific to clients with anxiety. Their basic idea is that clinicians who operate on the basis of standard cognitive conceptualizations of anxiety may fail to recognize that some clients may feel overwhelmed by a rapid increase in their feelings of impending danger when confronted with an anxiety-provoking situation. Clinicians who recognize this key element should be able to adjust their interventions by helping clients think differently about their appraisals of threat. Researchers have also provided potentially useful information relevant to particular therapies and client problems. For example, completing homework assignments appears particularly important for success in cognitive-behavioral therapies (Mash & Hunsley, 1993); Burns and Nolen-Hoeksema (1991) found that clients who did homework improved three times as much as those who did not. Foa and colleagues (1983) established that in working with phobic clients, limited habituation to feared stimuli during treatment sessions lead to treatment failure and that depression seemed to heighten clients' reactivity to feared stimuli and led to limited habituation.

Mash and Hunsley (1993) offered an important suggestion for the reconceptualization of failing clients. They recommended that clinicians dealing with treatment failure refocus their conceptualizations on short-term and intermediate outcomes. Clinicians should consider such intermediate indicators as the failure to implement treatment adequately (i.e., *treatment fidelity* and strength), the quality of the working alliance, and the client's motivation, noncompliance, degree of self-disclosure, problems with affect, and skill in verbal communication. Difficulties in these areas, Mash and Hunsley suggest, may be evident in as little as three sessions. Mash and Hunsley also noted that researchers have found that clinician errors in application of techniques and structuring of treatment sessions are associated with treatment failure. In group therapy, intermediate outcomes include the degree of cohesiveness and the degree of structure.

Beyond the simple failure to make progress are research findings indicating that individual and group counseling can harm participants. For example, Lieberman, Yalom, and Miles (1973) studied 18 different encounter groups to identify characteristics of helpful and harmful leaders. Helpful leaders were high in caring and meaning attributions (e.g., interpretations, explanations) and moderate in providing emotional stimulation and executive functions (e.g., rules). On the other hand, harmful leaders were more aggressive, authoritarian, showed little respect for members, confronted frequently, and were highly self-disclosive.

SUMMARY AND CAUTIONS

Although the presence of a good case conceptualization may lead to a successful outcome, it does not guarantee it. And a poor conceptualization does not preclude general, positive effects in therapy. Faust (1986) noted that poor judgment about the causes of client problems may prevent the clinician from intervening effectively with a specific problem; that poor judgment, however, does not prevent the client from improving or benefiting in other ways. A clinician who fails to recognize that the cause of a client's social phobia results from certain irrational beliefs nevertheless may increase the client's social reinforcement (by meeting regularly) and sense of self-esteem (by forming a working alliance and listening well to that client). Although better and worse conceptualizations exist, the clinician's goal should not be to find a single true conceptualization or diagnosis. Instead, it is likely that the clinician will find multiple pathways to positive outcomes. One interpretation of the consistent finding in the psychotherapy outcome literature of relatively equal effects across therapeutic approaches (Smith & Glass, 1977) is that different types of interventions may be effective with the same client. This implies that different conceptualizations may also be useful for the same client and that different interventions with the same client will produce multiple outcomes, some of which overlap across treatment approaches and some of which are unique to particular treatment approaches. The most useful philosophy of conceptualization, then, may be to seek a model that contributes to desired positive outcomes and averts negative side-effects.

The approach described here is more constructivist than positivist. For two reasons, the absolute historical accuracy of a case formulation or problem etiology should be a secondary concern. First, it is simply not possible to independently assess the veracity of many reports of past events. Second, to a significant extent human beings construct memories, rather than recall them like data retrieved from computer files (see Lewinsohn & Rosenbaum, 1987). For example, the emphasis over the reality of past sexual abuse reported by some clients may be somewhat misplaced. These are individuals experiencing considerable pain, and the importance of the conceptualization about the source of their pain rests primarily on its ability to help guide a treatment that alleviates that distress—not on the historical accuracy of whether the abuse did or did not occur.

Clinicians may wish to share or codevelop the conceptualization with the client (e.g., Needleman, 1999). JCAHO Guidelines (1997), for example, indicate that clients should be encouraged to participate in the creation of treatment plans. Several considerations apply here. Because sharing or cocreating a conceptualization with a client can be considered an intervention, the timing of this activity may depend upon the specific client. Some clients may not be able to easily understand concepts from certain therapeutic perspectives and would benefit from related instruction, further explanations, and experiences related to the concepts (Berman, 1997). Another option is to construct or translate the conceptualization into the language of a therapeutic approach that the client can better understand (Needleman, 1999); the tenets of transactional analysis, for example, may be more comprehensible to the average client than the intricacies of object relations theory. Such a translation ensures that the client can consider the treatment steps that follow from the conceptualization. Although learning about case conceptualization can often appear relatively straightforward to clinical instructors, in practice it can be complex (Meier, 1999). Students often find it difficult, for example, to translate abstract theories into procedural knowledge with specific clients (Binder & Strupp, 1997; Nelson & Neufeldt, 1998). My experience as an instructor has been that although conceptualization guidelines and client examples provide students with an adequate introduction, students can make fundamental mistakes on their first attempts at client models. Because instructors should not assume skilled performance, they should frequently review student models and provide feedback. As homework, I typically ask students to provide a photocopy of models for one or more clients and then provide written comments on that work. In addition to instructor feedback, students working in small groups can provide each other with useful feedback about models' parsimony, potential alternative explanations, and the quality of figures and diagrams. Once students are familiar with the principles of model creation and evaluation, they may be encouraged to conduct brief literature reviews related to their conceptualization and to determine if relevant empirically validated treatments exist (e.g., Linehan, 1993).

⁂THREE⁂

CLINICAL ASSESSMENT

———•◦•———

The interest is to help people to learn how to . . . advocate articulately what they deeply believe in, yet simultaneously encourage inquiry, especially about whatever they are advocating.

— Argyris (1976, p. 640)

Science is not a collection of facts, any more than opera is a collection of notes. It's a process, a way of thinking, based on a single insight—that the degree to which an idea seems true has nothing to do with whether it is true, and that the way to distinguish factual ideas from false ones is to test them.

— Ferris (1998, p. 5)

Although "intervention cannot be effective without some form of assessment" (Cone, 1989, p. 1241), clinical observation and judgment can be implicit and unsystematic (see Garb, 1998). Nierenberg and Mulroy (1997) observed that most clinicians do not use measurement to determine treatment response, but rather, employ a "more impressionistic assessment of improvement" (p. 19). Thus, Faust (1986) suggests that "assessment techniques may be effective to the extent that they reduce freedom to vary methods of data collection and combination on the basis of subjective impressions, or to the extent that they reduce or eliminate the role of human judgment" (p. 424).

One goal of this book is to provide sufficient systematicity to clinical assessment that the resulting data, though flawed, may prove useful in the analysis stage of the feedback loop. Clinical assessment is the vehicle for providing data that can be employed for such purposes as evaluating therapeutic progress, the usefulness of the case conceptualization, and the usefulness of the assessments themselves (Kazdin, 1993).

Although the importance of feedback is at least implicitly recognized in contemporary emphases on outcome assessment, the potentially useful role of qualitative and quantitative data in the clinical process has often been neglected. Research suggests that only 20% of psychologists collect outcome data (Clement, 1999). Historically, many clinical authors have not addressed assessment, but instead, have focused primarily on the etiology of client problems and intervention options. Clinical theorists who provide definitions of key clinical constructs, and then build on those definitions to create qualitative or quantitative assessments, are rare. Among such theorists are Gottman and Leiblum (1974; see also Kazdin, 1993), who recommended continuous monitoring of treatment progress so that the resulting data could be used for feedback relevant to treatment decisions. In contemporary inpatient treatment, one of the most effective approaches is a social learning model that depends heavily on frequent assessment of clients for feedback about treatment effectiveness (Paul & Menditto, 1992). Similarly, Clement (1999, p. 13) maintained that "when a therapist gives regular feedback on how a patient is doing, the patient improves more than when such feedback is not provided." Clement provided an example of clients improving while on a waiting list because they completed a weekly BDI before beginning treatment.

GENERAL MEASUREMENT PRINCIPLES

Measurement refers to the process of assigning numbers or categories to represent a phenomenon according to agreed upon rules (Krantz, Luce, Suppes, & Tversky, 1971). The rules represent a theory about how to measure phenomena of interest. The practical application of those rules occurs with *tests*, that is, systematic procedures for observing some aspect of human behavior and describing it using a numerical scale or category system (Cronbach, 1984). *Assessment* is a broader term than *tests*, referring to a human judge's combination of data from tests and other sources, such as interviews (see Aftanas, 1994). The phenomenon of interest is termed a *construct*, which is an abstract summary of natural regularities indicated by observable events. Psychological phenomena of clinical interest are indicated not usually by a single event but by a pattern of behaviors or occurrences that we connect together to specify the construct.

In this chapter, the primary focus will be on the use of tests and assessments applicable to individuals, couples, groups, and families in clinical contexts. Two traditional methods of evaluating the quality of all tests and assessments are described next.

Reliability

This refers to the consistency of scores produced by a test or assessment procedure. Traditionally, if one administers a test measuring a stable psychological trait (such as IQ) to a group of individuals, and later readministers the same test to the same group, the scores on the two administrations should be highly correlated (e.g., above .80; see Meier & Davis, 1990). If the scores are uncorrelated, questions arise as to whether the test can be appropriately used with this group to produce trustworthy information.

In clinical settings, two circumstances complicate the evaluation of a measure's reliability: the nature of the constructs being assessed and the small number of individuals or pieces of data being evaluated. Many clinical constructs are focused not on relatively stable personality or intellectual *traits* but psychological *states* that usually vary over short periods of time, such as anxiety or depression (Meier, 1997, 1998). Table 3.1 displays traditional methods for evaluating reliability.

Most of these methods were developed for the purposes of evaluating stable personality traits measured via multiple item tests. Evaluation of reliability with state tests should focus not on the temporal stability of an assessment but on the degree to which the procedure produces stable data at a specific point in time. For example, if a clinician listens to a tape of a therapy session to count client statements related to anxiety, that count is reliable if the same count is reproduced when the clinician (or another listener or rater) listens to the tape a second time. Methods of evaluating reliability with clinical measures will be discussed further in Chapter 5.

Table 3.1   Traditional Methods for Evaluating Measurement Reliability

Method	Description
Split-half reliability	Extent to which two halves of the same test correlate
Internal consistency/ Coefficient alpha	Average correlation between any item and the sum of the items
Alternate-form reliability	Correlation between two forms of the same test
Test-retest reliability	Correlation between two administrations of the same test given to the same persons
Interrater reliability	Correlation between two raters who observe the same phenomenon

Table 3.2   Traditional Methods for Evaluating Measurement Validity

Method	Description
Face validity	The extent to which test item content matches the apparent purpose of the test
Content validity	Whether the content of a test taps into all of a construct's important domains
Predictive validity	The degree to which a test can predict future performance on a criterion
Construct validity	Whether a test measures the construct it is intended to measure; the inferences for which a test's scores can be employed

Validity

Test and assessment data are valid if they (a) reflect the construct they are intended to measure and (b) provide data useful for a particular purpose. All tests are intended to measure particular constructs such as intelligence or anxiety. Interpretation of scores on those tests are intended for different purposes, including selection (for admission to schools or for different jobs) and detecting change (resulting from an educational or psychological intervention). Traditional approaches to evaluating validity are displayed in Table 3.2.

Construct validity is considered of primary importance. Historically, construct validity refers to whether a test measures the construct it is intended to measure (Meier, 1994). A more contemporary definition of construct validity refers to the inferences for which a test's scores can be employed. In other words, what evidence is there that the test can be employed for a particular purpose? One approach to evaluating construct validity (Campbell & Fiske, 1959) is to examine *convergent validity* (i.e., the extent to which two similar tests of the same construct correlate) and *discriminant validity* (the extent to which two tests of the same construct, but measured with different methodologies, correlate).

Contemporary measurement theorists note that all tests have *multiple validities*, that is, different factors that influence scores on a test (Wiley, 1991). Tests with high validity reflect more of the factor of interest; a test measuring depression, for example, should differentiate among persons with varying levels of depression but not necessarily distinguish among persons of varying intelligence. Tests and assessments with low validity are likely to be influenced by several sources of error. A universal, usually undesired error on all tests and assessments is *method variance*, that portion of the test score attributable to the method of obtaining data (Campbell & Fiske, 1959). In other words, how data are obtained always influences the resulting scores. In addition, issues such as *reactivity* (the transparency of a measure, which allows the test taker to know the intent of the test), *acquiescence* (responding "yes" to all items regardless of content), *socially desirable responding* (answering questions to present oneself in a favorable light), and *factors in the test environment* (e.g., computer-administered tests, characteristics of the test administrator) may interfere with valid responding.

COMMON TYPES OF ASSESSMENTS AND TESTS

To measure constructs of interests, clinicians must choose among a variety of types of assessments and tests. The problem, of course, is that few rules are available to guide choices among these methods in clinical settings. One result of this situation is that many clinicians tend to default to traditional measures or ones with which they are most familiar. The major categories of clinical interest include self-reports, ratings by others, behavioral observation, projective techniques, psychophysiological recording, qualitative assessment, and constructivist assessment. These categories are described below.

Self-Reports

These are judgments made by individuals about some personal psychological characteristic (e.g., rate your current level of anxiety). Because of their ease of use and inexpensiveness, self-reports are the usual choice for assessing clinical constructs (see Piotrowski, 1996). For example, Babor, Stephens, and Marlatt (1987; see also Babor, Brown, & Del Boca, 1990) noted that self-reports have been employed in alcohol research since the beginning of the 20th century and that verbal reports remain "the procedure of choice for obtaining research data about patient characteristics and the effectiveness of alcoholism treatment" (p. 412). What is true in alcohol treatment research remains true in most other clinical areas: Self-reports remain popular.

Despite the widespread use of self-reports, many clinicians and clinical researchers often adopt one of the following beliefs: (a) because individuals can self-report, self-reports must be valid, or (b) because self-reports can be distorted, self-reports are useless (Meier, 1994). As noted in Chapter 1, another interesting problem with self-reports is the assumption that items have the same meaning across individuals (see Schwarz, 1999). That is, clinical researchers typically assume that everyone understands self-report items in the same way. Based on clinical experience that shows that clients interpret similar life events in very different ways, this largely untested assumption is likely to be incorrect.

Ratings By Others

These are qualitative and quantitative judgments made by one person about another, which include interviews and clinical rating scales. Because "people behave in ways that are discrepant from their self-perceptions," outside observers add "unique and independent observation" (Kerig, 2001, p. 2). For example, a number of systems have been developed to observe and rate families and their members (Kerig & Lindahl, 2001) and psychotherapy groups (Beck & Lewis, 2000). Such observations, however, are expensive. One estimate indicated that 20 hours are needed to code 1 hour of family interactions (Gottman, 1979, cited in Kerig, 2001).

Employed to assess changes in interaction following family therapy, the Structural Family Systems Ratings (SFSR; Robbins, Hervis, Mitrani, & Szapocznik, 2001) is based on Minuchin's structural theory that states that patterns of communication create family structures (see Fiese et al., 2001, for a similar system focused on family narratives). Over a 3-month period of 6 hours per week, raters are trained to identify five dominant interaction patterns: *structure* (i.e., leadership, alliances, communication flow), *developmental state* (parenting roles, child roles and tasks), *resonance* (differentiation, enmeshment, disengagement), *identified patient* (negativity, centrality), and *conflict resolution* (denial, avoidance, diffusion, resolution). The assessment occurs as part of a family task where members are seated so that they can talk with one another. A video camera tapes all members while they complete three separate tasks that take about 5 to7 minutes each (e.g., members decide on a meal that they all would enjoy eating). Robbins and colleagues (2001) found evidence supporting interrater reliability, test-retest reliability, internal consistency, and content validity for SFSR scales.

Goal Attainment Scaling (GAS) is primarily an evaluation tool designed to assess the degree of change in a group of clients receiving treatment from a program (Kiresuk & Sherman, 1968; Kiresuk et al., 1994). Typically, five steps are involved:

1. Create at least three goals for the client.

2. Select an indicator of each goal (e.g., crying, to indicate depression).

3. Specify an expected outcome for each goal (i.e., what treatment is likely to produce) in terms of particular criteria (e.g., client cries only one time a week).

4. Specify levels of outcome for each goal that are somewhat more and somewhat less than expected.

5. Specify levels of outcome for each goal that are much more and much less than expected (for a total of five plausible levels of outcome).

Levels of outcome should be stated in scale points such that "the presence or absence of which can be easily judged by a follow-up worker who has had no contact with the clinical or therapeutic procedures of the treatment unit" (Kiresuk & Sherman, 1968, p. 447).

GAS scores are not normative; for example, an individual can improve a great deal on a GAS scale but still possess a level of skills or behaviors on that GAS scale that is relatively dysfunctional when compared to the level of others' skills or behaviors. Also, GAS scores are not behavioral: The amount of change is not linked to a behavior or criterion. Kiresuk and colleagues report that typically client and therapist set goals collaboratively and that research and clinical experience suggest this fosters a better outcome. They also recommend that an independent, trained rater conduct the follow-up evaluation.

Finally, Clement (1994) described a simple system for outcome assessment where the clinician rates the client on the following 5-point scale:

1. Much worse than at intake

2. Worse than at intake

3. No change from intake to termination

4. Improved

5. Much improved

Like the Global Assessment of Functioning scale (GAF), the major benefit of such a broad rating is its economy.

Behavioral Observation

This refers to assessments of overt behavior, which are often performed by a trained rater. Although the difference between behavioral observation and ratings by others can be subtle, depending on the procedure, behavioral observation usually involves direct observation of client behaviors (e.g., counting how many times a client cries during a session), whereas ratings by others requires an evaluation of behavior on some type of rating scale (e.g., degree of depression).

A recent special issue of *Psychological Assessment* was devoted to different forms of clinically relevant *analogue behavioral observations*. Often developed for research purposes, these assessments involve "the observation of clients (e.g., individual children and adults, families, couples) in an environment that is designed to increase the chance that the assessor can observe clinically important behavior and interactions" (Haynes, 2001, p. 3). Haynes (2001) notes that the assessor structures the environment to simulate problematic situations or to manipulate variables likely to be controlling client behavior.

The resulting behaviors, observations, and data can increase the quality of the assessment procedure and provide information relevant to understanding process-outcome relations in the client or clients. Domains include observing interactions between parents and children with externalizing disorders (Roberts, 2001); fear, avoidance, and hyperactivity acts performed in children (Mori & Armendariz, 2001); social anxiety and skills deficits in adults (Norton & Hope, 2001); and conflict in couples (Heyman, 2001). Role-plays, for example, can be used with clients "to reconstruct threatening situations, demonstrate emotional reactions, elicit motor response sequences, reconstruct the client's self-talk, and observe symptomatic behaviors" (Mash & Foster, 2001, p. 93; see Kanfer & Schefft, 1988).

Self-monitoring can be considered a combination of behavioral observation and self-report where clients observe and record their clinically relevant behaviors. Recording of such behavioral problems as smoking has been shown to decrease that behavior independent of other interventions (see, e.g., Gottman & Leiblum, 1974; Lichstein, 1970; Nelson, 1977a, 1977b). Any client behavior could potentially be self-monitored both to obtain assessment data and function as an additional intervention. Behavioral observation of others' behavior may also result in changes in those behaviors. In a study of the effects of measurement, Bloom, Hursh, Wienke, and Wolf (1992) found that, compared to baseline conditions, teachers' frequent measurement and graphing of targeted student behaviors resulted in improvements in those behaviors. These results were found regardless of whether the teachers employed paper-and-pencil or computer systems for measurement, although teachers indicated that they preferred the computer methods and more frequently altered their interventions when they used the computer. Teachers continued to record data regularly, using the computer method, following the formal study.

Bloom and colleagues suggested that one explanation for these results is that data collection helped teachers to focus on the specific objectives for behavior change with their students. Data collection concerning "complying with requests," for example, focused the teacher's attention on the student's action following the request as well as the reinforcers the teacher employed with that student. Similarly, students often had an increased awareness of their specific behaviors when monitored. Bloom and colleagues also found that teachers employed the resulting data to make decisions about their interventions with students. They concluded "the type of intervention chosen may be a moot point unless student progress is monitored" (p. 189). Thus, self-monitoring and observation of others' behavior may both change behavior because of the feedback provided.

Projective Techniques

These include measures that attempt to reveal intrapsychic issues through the presentation of ambiguous stimuli. Projectives tend to be used less as measures of change than as indicators of information about unconscious processes and structures. The most well-known projective device, the Rorschach, was published in 1921 and developed to assist in differentiating between normal and clinical groups (Groth-Marnat, 1990). The Rorschach consists of 10 cards with symmetrical inkblots. The examiner hands the card to the subject and asks "What might this be?" The examiner continues through all 10 cards and records the free association the respondent makes for each card. After this initial sequence, the examiner again goes through each card, asking the respondent to indicate the material on the card that stimulated the particular responses. Although the Rorschach is the predominant projective technique, many clinical researchers have very different perspectives about its reliability and validity (see Garb, Florio, & Grove, 1998; Parker, Hanson, & Hunsley, 1988). Continued use of the Rorschach projective test may partially result from its perceived utility in providing information relevant to individualizing case conceptualization and treatments (Viglione, 1999).

Psychophysiological Recording

This refers to measures that quantify biological and physiological events related to psychological functioning. The use of these measures depends on the link between a physiological state and an educational or psychological construct (Cacioppo & Tassinary, 1990; Matarazzo, 1992). For example, we might suppose that occupational stress would be correlated with measures such as heart rate or blood pressure. Moreover, because indicators such as heart rate or blood pressure are not subject to voluntary control, they function as objective measures of clinical processes and outcomes. Historically, psychophysiological measures have been more expensive than self-reports and ratings of others, and consequently they have been used less frequently in clinical settings.

The phenomenon of *desynchrony* frequently appears during measurement with multiple psychophysiological measures. Desynchrony occurs when systems that seemingly should be correlated are not (Lang, 1968; Rachman &

Hodgson, 1974). For example, an individual who perceives a feared object such as a snake may show an elevated heart rate but stable or decreasing blood pressure. Similarly, one of the interesting results of psychotherapy with individuals is that outcomes may be desynchronous: Measures of cognition and affect in an individual may show improvement, for example, but the individual's behavior does not change.

Qualitative Assessment

This refers to procedures that produce or collect a broad range of non-numerical data, such as language and graphics. Qualitative assessors typically observe individuals or present them with queries designed to elicit samples of the phenomenon in question. Qualitative assessment also refers to the process of observers recording the occurrence of specified target behaviors in therapy and the events that occur immediately before and after those behaviors (Haynes et al., 1993). And, as discussed later in this chapter, therapy progress notes can be seen as a qualitative material for subsequent analysis.

Silverman, Ricci, and Gunter (1990) note that

> while bias can be an important negative factor in quantitative research, it is a particular danger in qualitative research, in which the researcher typically immerses him- or herself in the field situation, has substantial flexibility in selecting and categorizing "key" elements from a wealth of rich and detailed data, and has considerable latitude in the interpretation and analysis of data. (p. 71)

They recommend a combination of increased structure and a standardized approach to qualitative methods, including the use of semistructured interviews (while retaining some flexibility in the interview process), systematic sampling of persons, obtaining data from different sources to balance biases, and obtaining documents to validate the qualitative themes found in the interviews.

As examples of qualitative assessments that could be clinically relevant, Goldman (1992) described the Life Line and the Vocational Card Sort (VCS). For the Life Line, clients first draw a line vertically along a sheet of paper and then begin to list important life events along the line chronologically. The VCS consists of a set of cards containing occupational names that the client sorts in two stages. First, the cards are sorted into three piles: occupations that the person would *consider*, would *not consider*, and has *doubts* about. Next, clients take the piles, beginning with the *not consider* category, and sorts them into smaller piles containing similar reasons the person would not consider them. This exploration process enables clinician and client to get an in-depth sense of the factors important to the client's career decision making.

Constructivist Assessment

Proponents of constructivist assessment believe that humans construct their psychological realities and that it is the linguistic constructions of individual persons—instead of the test developer—that should be measured (Boeker et al., 2000; Meier, 1994; Neimeyer & Neimeyer, 1993). This type of assessment is based on the work of George Kelly (1955), who developed a theory of personal constructs. Kelly proposed that constructs are bipolar distinctions (i.e., expressions of opposites) that enable the perceiver to construct discrete meanings out of the vast amount of perceivable stimuli (Neimeyer & Neimeyer, 1993). Constructivist proponents believe that meaning is constructed through language organized into narratives, metaphors, and stories (Sarbin, 1986).

Constructivists examine interconnected constructs through *repertory grid techniques* (Beail, 1985; Kelly, 1955; Neimeyer, 1993). These techniques are typically administered in an interview, in which individuals select elements from a personal domain (e.g., potential careers such as construction worker, park ranger, and electrical engineer) and then rate those elements on personally selected constructs (e.g., low or high starting salary, indoor or outdoor work, low or high opportunity for advancement). Neimeyer, Brown, Metzler, Hagans, and Tanguy (1989) maintained that research has demonstrated that individuals process personally selected constructs and constructs provided by others in fundamentally different ways (as with items in nomothetic tests). As idiographic proponents would argue, constructs created by individuals carry greater personal meaning and thereby facilitate greater understanding and more accurate recall of vocational information. The content and numeric ratings produced in repertory grid techniques provide qualitative and quantitative information for subsequent analysis (Neimeyer, 1988, 1989a, 1989b).

OTHER METHODS

Several other types of assessments and tests, which are infrequently employed in clinical settings and yet potentially of great use, do not fit well into the preceding categories. These measures are described below.

Analysis of Speech Acts

This method focuses on the types and structure of normal and disrupted spoken language during therapy (Greenberg, 1986; Madill et al., 2001; Mahl, 1987). As computer software and hardware develop to handle the recording and analysis of speech acts more effortlessly, analysis of spoken language during therapy and assessment appears likely to increase in frequency and importance in clinical practice.

Community and Epidemiological Assessment

In these assessments, the groups of interests are entire communities. Relevant concepts include *morbidity rates*, *incidence rates* (i.e., new cases of a disorder divided by the total population), and *prevalence rates* (i.e., total number of cases divided by total population) (Higgs & Gustafson, 1985).

Simulations

These are contrived situations designed to provide clients with stimuli similar to real-life problems. Analogues or simulations may be computer-based (Meier & Wick, 1991), presented in laboratory settings, or simple role-playing between therapists and clients (Haynes, 2001).

Mapping Procedures

These include data collection methods that involve graphics. Mattaini (1993) described *ecomaps* (graphic tools for showing family-environment transactions; Hartman, 1978), *genograms* (graphic family trees used to portray the intergenerational life and relationships in a family structural mapping; Minuchin, 1974), *family mapping* (that depicts current relationships within a household), *time or life lines* (which show significant events across time on a single dimension), and *social support mapping* (that uses a graphic to display individuals important in a client's life and their relative closeness, interrelationships, and type of support).

RULING OUT METHODS

Although it may not be possible to designate a particular method as the single best approach for clinical assessment, some methods may be inappropriate for

Table 3.3   Sources of Information for Four Assessment Methods

		Method	
Self-Report	*Ratings By Others*	*Behavioral Observations*	*Qualitative Assessment*
Client	Clinician	Client	Client
	Significant other	Trained observer	Significant other
	Staff	Staff Clinician	Staff Clinician

use with particular clients. Table 3.3 below illustrates four methods and their typical sources of information. While by definition self-reports are provided by the client, other methods can be completed by a variety of sources.

Particularly when considering the use of self-reports and ratings by others, determine whether clients have the necessary *cognitive skills* (e.g., sufficient knowledge about the content area), *emotional states* (e.g., sufficient motivation), and *environmental conditions* (e.g., privacy, quiet surroundings, ability to operate equipment such as computers) to adequately perform assessment tasks (Meier, 1994). For example, some assessors avoid self-reports with schizophrenics and depressed individuals because those groups can experience difficulty providing reliable information (Neufeld, 1977). Similarly, a parent going through a divorce or in the midst of a custody battle may be biased in reports of his or her own and others' parenting behaviors.

To the extent that a client's cognitive abilities and skills differ from assessment requirements and purposes—because of language or cultural differences, lack of education and cognitive skills, or insufficient knowledge—problems may occur in interpreting subsequent data (Meier, 1994). For example, when the gap between the language used in test items and clients' cognitive abilities is sufficiently large, objective test items become ambiguous stimuli; the resulting item response is likely to be a generation, rather than recall, of information. If clients are children whose reading level precludes them from fully understanding self-report items, it is reasonable to assume that they may guess on such items. Even clients who should reasonably be expected to be able to provide valid information may not do so. For example, Schwarz (1999) summarized research that indicates that when asked to report information, people typically do not retrieve all the applicable knowledge. Instead, they tend to recall information that is chronically accessible, that is, information that comes to mind whenever the person thinks about it. In contrast, some information is temporarily accessible, that is, it comes to mind when a context or situation prompts the person to recall it. One of those contexts is preceding items. Strack, Schwarz, and Gschneidinger (1985) instructed respondents to recall three positive or three negative events. Those who reported positive events subsequently indicated higher life satisfaction than those who reported negative events.

A client's affective states will also influence performance on clinical assessments. Unmotivated individuals may answer randomly or employ a response style such as acquiescence. On the other hand, highly motivated test takers may fake good or bad or employ a response set such as socially desirable responding. Brody and Forehand (1986) found that depressed mothers were more likely than mothers with low depression to interpret their children's noncompliant behavior as indicative of maladjustment. Schwarz (1999) summarized research that found that individuals' retrospective reports of emotion were more intense than their reports of current emotions (e.g., Parkinson, Briner, Reynolds, & Totterdell, 1995). This may be due to the reference period employed by respondents; Schwarz (1999) noted that current reports typically refer to one day or so, whereas retrospective reports request information about longer periods. Respondents may infer that the questioner, when referring to a briefer period, is interested in more frequent events and, when referring to a longer period, is interested in more infrequent (and possibly, intense) events. It is also possible that with more time respondents feel more comfortable holding the intense emotions in consciousness (i.e., there is less repression).

Finally, factors in the test environment, such as the presence of observers, the use of computer-based tests or other special equipment, and the characteristics of test administrators, have the potential for influencing assessment-related behaviors. Even individuals who have appropriate cognitive skills and motivation (e.g., few concerns about doing well or behaving properly) may restrict or alter their responses until they become accustomed to any unusual aspects of the testing environment.

UNITS OF MEASUREMENT

In addition to decisions about what type of assessment or test to employ, clinicians must choose one or more units of measurement, as different qualities and

Table 3.4   Units of Measurement Used for Assessment Methods

Qualitative Assessment	Self-Report/Ratings By Others	Behavioral Observations
Themes	Frequency counts	Frequency counts
Stories	Intensity	Amount of time
Issues	Severity	Activity level
Type of intervention	Amount of change	Event presence/absence

quantities can be collected within each method. Table 3.4 displays some of these dimensions, arranged by type of assessment.

Frequency counts involve simple tabulations of the number of times something happens. The something can be as simple as a discrete behavior (e.g., smoking one cigarette) or as complex an occurrence as an emotion experienced. For example, clinicians frequently encounter clients who experience considerable difficulty expressing affect. With such clients a useful outcome might be to increase affective self-disclosures. Particularly if audio-taping is possible, a clinician might assess the construct of affective self-disclosure by counting such disclosures each session; examples of affective disclosures include grief about a parent's death, stress about being over-worked, or happiness about beginning a new relationship. A clinician might also be interested in recording the type of interventions that occurred in each session. For example, in structured groups it is common practice to employ different exercises or address different themes each week. If the case conceptualization included a hypothesis about which type of exercise had a greater impact on group process, it would be important to record that type of exercise.

The choice of unit of measurement does have implications for the quality of the resulting data. If the clinician defaults to a global rating scale, as discussed later in this chapter, the resulting data may be influenced by factors other than the intended construct (see Bond, Bloch, & Yalom, 1979). In general, more specific units of measurement produce better data (Paul, 1986). Particular clients may also provide information more amenable to assessment with particular methods. When a client frequently uses metaphors and tells stories, recording the themes contained in them is useful. However, resources often dictate which of these methods is employed: Global ratings, for example, usually require considerably less effort than do frequency counts.

CREATING A CLINICAL ASSESSMENT

As discussed in Chapter 1, many clinical researchers (Bickman et al., 2000; Cone, 1988; Kiresuk et al., 1994; Mash & Hunsley, 1993) agree that idiographic measures are needed that (a) are sensitive to the specific behaviors of individual clients and (b) can be changed during the course of treatment. These assessments should also be brief and relatively inexpensive (as a result of being focused on the targets of change) and easily modified (or dropped, if treatment goals change). When clinicians are deciding on methods for assessment and testing, however, these objectives must be balanced with available resources (see Mash & Foster, 2001). Clinical assessment can be expensive in terms of staff and client time, the clerical resources necessary to collect and store assessment data, and the cost of purchasing commercially published tests or software for scoring or data analysis.

While treatment failure has been previously described as an instance necessitating the use of as many resources as possible, other situations exist where more than the usual resources are typically expended on assessment tasks. These include (a) clinical training where students complete conceptualization, assessment, and analysis tasks with their clients (which may range from one client to all clients in their caseload) and (b) clinicians in agencies and settings who value a science-practice approach and view the feedback loop of conceptualization, assessment, and analysis of intervention effects as a professional standard (see, e.g., Gray & Lambert, 2001).

With this background in mind, four steps are described below that are useful in creating an idiographic clinical assessment. These steps provide a degree of structure that enables a more systematic collection of clinically relevant data (Mash & Foster, 2001).

The steps are:

Begin with the case conceptualization.

Explicate constructs.

Measure behaviors.

Collect as much data as possible.

BEGIN WITH THE CASE CONCEPTUALIZATION

The client's presenting problem provides information about desired outcomes, while the client's description of relevant history and events indicates potential causes for the client's problems. As described in Chapter 2, the construction of the case conceptualization enables the clinician to identify key process and selected outcome elements for assessment; recall Luke, whose outcomes of interest were anxiety and sleep problems. The number of these elements to be assessed, discussed below, is usually influenced by the available resources and norms of the particular practice settings.

In no instance, however, should a construct not included in the case conceptualization be assessed. Occasionally, a clinician will find that she or he is measuring something important but not formally addressed in the model. If the measured construct is in fact important for a particular client, the conceptualization should be reevaluated and the assessed element included in the client model. Unless the case conceptualization and assessment elements are closely connected, the resulting data cannot be used to inform decisions about interventions based on that conceptualization.

EXPLICATE CONSTRUCTS

The basic idea of construct explication is for the clinician to specify, as clearly as possible, how the constructs of interest for a particular client should be observed, measured, or assessed. This is a surprisingly difficult and often ignored task. Many clinicians take an implicitly nomothetic stance to assessment, assuming that clinically related constructs can be measured in the same way for all clients, typically with self-reports or ratings by others.

Because global ratings appear susceptible to certain types of bias (Hill, 1991), the goal in construct explication is to select or create assessments that are as concrete and specific as possible. To do so, Hartman (1984) proposed six steps to follow when creating an assessment for a process or outcome element in a client model:

1. *Assign a general name to the construct.* For example, the client's major outcome might be anxiety.

2. *Define the construct.* For a particular client with anxiety, anxiety might best be defined as a cognitive and affective state experienced before the occurrence of a potentially threatening event. For others, the anxiety might be more generalized or free floating and not easily tied to any specific event.

3. *Elaborate on the critical components of behavior that define the construct.* Anxiety might occur when a client begins to think about an anticipated aversive event, at which point the anxiety is primarily manifested through verbal and nonverbal behaviors.

4. *Provide typical examples.* For instance, the client begins to pull her hair, increases her fidgeting, stutters slightly, and can report that she is feeling anxious.

5. *Describe questionable instances that may or may not be indicators of the construct.* For example, it might be that the client's finger tapping should not count as an instance of anxiety unless it is accompanied by self-report or other nonverbal indicators of anxiety.

6. *Describe the units of measurement.* For example, it may be useful to record *how many* times the client pulls her hair in a session, *how long* she can sit still without any body movement, or her *rating* of anxiety on a 1 to 10 scale.

These steps can be used to facilitate the explication of any construct in a client model. If you follow these steps and discover that the best method of measuring the construct is a standardized measure, then by all means use that measure. The more likely result of performing a construct explication, how-ever, is an assessment that is idiographic and behavioral. The issue of using nomothethic or standardized scales versus idiographic assessments is dis-cussed further below in *Low Resource Alternatives*.

When creating idiographic measures, write these steps out as a way of adding necessary structure to the process (also see the forms provided by Zuckerman, 1997). Simply choosing a measure without explicitly following these explication steps may result in confusion during the measurement process or confusion about the interpretation of the resulting data. Another example application of these steps is provided later in this chapter in Figure 3.2, explicating the construct of group cohesiveness.

Construct explication is similar to a researcher's operational definition of a construct except that clinical constructs are likely to be expressed through multiple operations. In other words, a researcher may define anxiety through a single operation (e.g., a total score on an anxiety self-report scale), but con-struct explication in a clinical setting should include that operation and any others that are pertinent to the client's manifestation of anxiety.

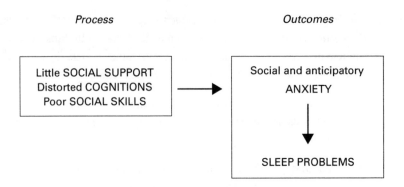

Low resource alternatives

Resources may be unavailable to allow the implementation of the 6 steps described above to assess each process and outcome element in the case conceptualization. Recall the initial case conceptualization of Luke created in Chapter 2:

This conceptualization contains three process elements (social support, distorted cognitions, and social skills) and two outcome elements (anxiety, sleep problems). In low resource situations, it may be impractical to explicate and measure all five constructs. What are low-cost alternatives for assessing these constructs?

Primarily for administrative and documentation purposes, many agencies and insurers routinely employ nomothetic outcome measures to examine treatment effectiveness for *groups* of clients. In these contexts, outcome is assessed quantitatively via self-report tests (Clement, 1999; Cone, 2001; Lambert, 1994; Lyons, Howard, O'Mahoney, & Lish, 1997; Strupp, Horowitz, & Lambert, 1997; VandenBos, 1996). Because of their ease of use by clients, measures such as the OQ-45 (Ogles, Lambert, & Masters, 1996; Lambert & Huefner, 1996) and the Symptom Checklist-90 (SCL-90) are the outcome assessments of choice for many clinicians in diverse settings. A review of the literature indicates that hundreds of such measures have been developed for outcome assessment (Burn & Payment, 2000; Clement, 1999; Fischer & Corcoran, 1994; Nugent et al., 2001). Many of these instruments were not developed to measure change, nor do they follow from a particular theory related to psychotherapeutic change. The major strength of many of these scales appears to be their face validity; that is, test titles and item content indicate that the instrument measures a construct of clinical interest (e.g., anxiety, assertiveness, depression, eating disorders, shyness, social support, substance abuse). The exception to this trend are clinically relevant and theory-driven measures, such as the Automatic Thoughts Questionnaire (related to cognitive therapy; Holland & Kendall, 1980), the Survey of Heterosexual Interactions (related to behavior therapy; Twentyman, Boland, & McFall, 1981), and more recent clinical measures related to Bandura's self-efficacy theory. Perhaps the best example of therapy-driven assessment is the set of measures employed with Paul's residential treatment approach. Paul and colleagues (Licht, Paul, & Power, 1986; Paul, 1986, 1987a, 1987b) specified the sources of treatment-related information, domains assessed, schedules of assessment, types of error to avoid, and units of observation.

Such nomothetic scales may be useful as explication of clinical constructs in two ways. First, many outcome constructs (e.g., depression, anxiety) can be considered general indicators of functioning or symptomatology. Some validity evidence supports use of total scores on scales like the OQ-45, GAF, COMPASS scales, and SCL-90 as measures of functioning (Howard, Brill, Lueger, & O'Mahoney, 1995; Strupp et al., 1997). These scales can thus function as *proxy measures* in place of more direct or complete measurement of specific constructs (see Nugent et al., 2001). Many of these scales also have basic norms; comparing a client's scores to these norms provides one basis for deciding whether the client's behavior is sufficiently equivalent to the norm group's average range to indicate that treatment is needed or has been successful. In addition, subscales or individual items in these nomothetic measures may be relevant to specific clients. Thus, you may need to employ only the OQ-45 items related to social role performance with a client whose major therapy goal is to improve social skills. In sum, nomothetic measures already routinely employed for administrative purposes can be used as a low-cost alternative for obtaining data relevant to individual clients.

Figure 3.1 contains an experimental scale, the Client Symptom and Functioning Rating scale (CSFR), which can be used as a quick, proxy measure. Although it is similar to the Global Assessment of Functioning scale (GAF; American Psychiatric Association, 1994), the CSFR may be a better measure for persons with less severe problems. A clinician or client could use this scale, for example, to produce daily, weekly, or monthly assessments of outcome in the psychological, social, or occupational/educational domains. The *DSM-IV* (American Psychiatric Association, 1994) also contains GAF-type scales that can be employed to rate relationships (e.g., in families), social functioning, and occupational functioning.

Rate SYMPTOMS and FUNCTIONING in these areas:

   (a) psychological (personal/emotional),
   (b) social (interpersonal), and
   (c) occupational/educational (work/school performance).

Ratings should be made on the basis of apparent symptoms and impairments in functioning. Assign a number on the basis of the following categories; if a score falls between levels, use .5 (e.g., 4.5).

   1 = Transient symptoms (e.g., brief worrying after conflict with co-worker) and/or
       Slight impairment in functioning (e.g., some procrastination with work tasks)
   2 = Mild symptoms (e.g., depressed affect) and/or
       Some difficulty in functioning (e.g., occasional work absences)
   3 = Moderate symptoms (e.g., flat affect) and/or
       Moderate difficulty in functioning (no enduring friendships or interpersonal intimacy)
   4 = Serious symptoms (e.g., suicidal, homicidal, abusive) and/or
       Serious impairment in functioning (frequent change of schools or loss of jobs)
   5 = Psychiatric symptoms (e.g., delusions, inappropriate behavior) and/or
       psychiatric functioning (currently hospitalized or strong candidate for hospitalization)

Client Initials _____

Psychological score   *Social score*   *Occupational/ Educational score*

Psychological   Social score = ___   Occupational/
score = __   Educational score = ____

Sum = ____

Figure 3.1   Client Symptom and Functioning Rating (Experimental)

As noted in Chapter 1, however, the use of nomothetic measures has its disadvantages. Clinical researchers have long recognized that any sizable group of clients contains significant variation (Battle et al., 1966); even individuals with identical diagnoses display considerable variation. Thus, the use of a nomothetic measure can lead to evaluating clients on irrelevant constructs (Kiresuk & Sherman, 1968) and, as indicated by Prochaska and DiClemente's stages of change theory (Velicer et al., 1996), nomothetic tests can indicate deterioration in individual cases when other records suggest stability or progress (Quayle & Moore, 1998). Kiresuk and Sherman (1968) concluded that "to rate all patients with regard to their anxiety level, sexual problems, and thought disorder, whether or not these variables had anything to do with the patient's reason for coming to the clinic, appears to be unreasonable and wasteful" (p. 444). In addition, some clinicians may be tempted to see measures referred to as "standardized" or "objective" as more valid and precise than is evidenced by research findings. For example, Lambert (1994) indicated that the choice of outcome measurement may be as important as the chosen treatment in determining the size of the found treatment effect. Even with well-known measures of depression, Lambert (1994) wrote that "meta-analytic results suggest that the most popular dependent measures used to assess depression following treatment provide reliably different pictures of change" (p. 85).

Other types of readily accessible information may be used as proxy measures. In alcohol and drug abuse clinics, for example, attendance records and blood samples may be routinely collected and thereby offer convenient outcome measures for the clinician. With school children, grades, attendance, and facility use (e.g., number of visits to the health office or referrals to the office for discipline problems) offer potentially useful measures. In individual therapy, attendance and billing records may be supplemented by records of how many times a client is late for or cancels a session. In group settings, such easily collected information as who sits where and who interacts with whom may be informative. Assessments should ideally flow from the elements of models, but resources may sometimes dictate that available measures first be employed as proxies for more costly assessments.

In some situations, construct explication is possible but not all indicators of the construct can be assessed because of resource constraints (Kerig, 2001). Here one or two of the full set of indicators may need to function as proxies for the whole set (see Cone, 1988; Gottman & Leiblum, 1974). In group psychotherapy, for example, group cohesiveness is a construct that appears to be multidimensional (see Yalom, 1995). Figure 3.2 contains an explication of the construct of cohesiveness. We might expect more cohesive groups, for

Construct Name: *Group Cohesiveness*

General definition:
Group's ability to function as a
    whole, to stick together

Elaboration that describes critical
    parts of behavior:
Group size, distress displayed,
    subgrouping, amount of
    participation, therapist
    perception of cohesiveness

Typical examples:
For subgrouping, one or two members
    dominate the group discussion
    during most of the session

Questionable instances:
If subgrouping occurs but members
    shift between cliques during a
    session, this does not indicate a
    problem with the subgrouping

Units of Measurement

Group Size
1 = Too few or too many (< 4 or >11)
2 = Acceptable range (5-10)

Distress Displayed
1 = Very high or very low
2 = Moderate

Subgrouping
1 = Significant (> 1 episode)
2 = Few or no cliques

Participation
1 = Restricted to a few clients
2 = Free, full (e.g., 75% talk)

Therapist Perception
1 = Low cohesiveness
2 = High cohesiveness

Figure 3.2   Explicating Group Cohesiveness

example, to (a) be small in number, but not too small (e.g., 5 to 10 persons), (b) have members with moderate levels of distress, (c) possess few or no subgroups, (d) enjoy the full participation of members, and (e) be perceived by the therapist (or therapists) as cohesive.

This explication of cohesiveness suggests that data be collected for five separate ratings (group size, distress displayed, subgrouping, amount of participation, therapist perception of cohesiveness), with the units of measurement specified (in the side box) for each indicator. Where resources allow, collecting data on the five indicators is optimal. This may not, however, be feasible in many clinical contexts, and a reasonable alternative is to select one or two of the most easily obtained indicators to function as proxies for cohesiveness. For example, group attendance could provide a quick account of group size, and an after-session qualitative or quantitative rating of therapist perception of cohesiveness could also be easily obtained.

Qualitative data found in clinical *progress notes* represent a second source of low-cost information relevant to case conceptualization constructs. Traditionally, clinicians have kept progress notes for each therapy session (see

American Psychological Association, 1993; Sommers-Flanagan & Sommers-Flanagan, 1999). Perhaps because few guidelines exist for the content of such notes, they typically take the form of a general narrative or lists of important content. However, Wiger (1999, p. 130) provided guidelines for progress notes, including descriptions of (a) how the session related to treatment plan objectives; (b) the interventions and techniques employed; (c) important clinical observations (e.g., client cognition, behavior, affect); (d) recent progress or setbacks; (e) the diagnostic signs still present or now absent; (f) the treatment goals, including intermediate goals, met at this time; (g) current medical necessity; (h) work being done outside the session; and (i) the client's current strengths and impairments. Qualitative notes may also be necessary to document such important information as reports of suicidal ideation, homicidal intent, or child abuse.

Progress notes can be used for a variety of purposes, including enhancing the clinician's credibility to the client, documenting service effectiveness, establishing baseline behaviors, enhancing communication with therapists if the client transferred, keeping therapy on track, and noting the client's progress in relation to the treatment plan (Wiger, 1999). For our purposes, qualitative data in progress notes can be a key source of information, particularly about process factors that influence client outcomes. Client themes, stories, issues, and metaphors all represent qualitative data of potential use as indicators of process and outcome elements in a case conceptualization. For example, an anxious client might express that affective state by frequently switching topics within and between sessions. A recording of these topics and related information might eventually provide data about when, how often, and why the client switches issues, thereby deepening the case conceptualization and providing more information relevant for subsequent intervention.

MEASURE BEHAVIORS

If resources are available, an emphasis on explicating constructs so that they can be measured as concretely as possible will often translate into assessment of behavior. Although a construct such as self-esteem may be appropriately assessed by asking clients to rate themselves on a numeric scale, a valid measure might also be a behavior such as how often a client initiates conversations with peers.

Behavioral observation is a particularly important assessment method for two reasons. First, research in behavioral assessment has found that in general, the more an observer has to interpret events, rather than simply record them, the lower reliability and validity estimates will be (Paul, 1986). Second, behavioral assessment typically requires greater resources than do methods such as client self-reports and therapist ratings. Emphasizing behavioral assessment principles can provide clinicians and clinical students with the additional motivation needed to gain experience with this approach.

Paul (1986) suggested that most assessments can be classified as one of two forms: Direct Observational Coding (DOCs) or Questionnaires, Inventories, Checklists, and Scales (QICS). With DOCs, an observer records a sample of overt behavior. A clinician might count the number of times a client says in session "I feel sad" or instruct clients to count the number of cigarettes they smoke daily. Both "I feel sad" and the number of cigarettes smoked are potentially observable to any recorder. QICS are scales in which the respondent or another person reports on the client's perceptions, moods, behaviors, attitudes, and so forth. Client ratings of the impact of a counseling session would be an example of a QICS assessment.

Both DOCs and QICS measure constructs. The difficulty with QICS, however, is that there can be ambiguous connections between constructs (e.g., depression) and scores on the assessments intended to measure those constructs (e.g., self-reports of depressive symptoms). For example, a daily log of how often a client experienced a sleep disturbance (e.g., a checkmark indicating disturbance or not in a diary completed upon awakening) would likely be a better assessment of depression than would a therapist rating of the frequency of sleep disturbance based on the client's recall in session (e.g., "1 = not at all, 2 = some, 3 = great deal"). Thus, frame assessments as a DOC if resources allow. If you have a choice between a Likert rating of a phenomenon and a presence/absence rating, the latter is preferable because it requires less judgment.

Again, the principle is that the more an observer has to interpret an event—rather than simply record it—the less valid the assessment will be (Paul, 1986). With more interpretation, assessment data may include the characteristics of the observers as well as the assessment task (Paul, 1986). This problem may occur with rating scales that contain adjectives and adverbs that require the assessor to make judgments about behavior. Paul (1986) notes that reliability and validity estimates of tests and assessments often improve when

			Client		
Session	*C^1*	*C^2*	*C^3*	*C^4*	*C^5*
1		A		A	
2				A	
3		A		A	
4		A		A	
5		A	A		
6	A	A	A	A	
7		A	A	A	
8				A	A

Figure 3.3   Absences in a Substance Abuse Group

NOTE: "C" means client; "A" indicates that the client was absent for that group session.

measurement moves away from natural language anchors and toward more specific behavioral and physical definitions. For these reasons, Paul (1986) concludes that DOCs possess better reliability and validity estimates than QICS. Thus, explicate constructs as a DOC if resources allow.

A very basic example of a DOC is attendance in a group. A student clinician who cofacilitated a group for substance abusers quickly developed the model below after observing frequent absences and changes in membership:

Although not a curative factor per se in most group models, frequent attendance is typically seen as a prerequisite for a good outcome (see Yalom, 1995). Given that the focus of this group was preventing relapse, the student reasoned that clients had to attend group before group process and content could influence drug use. He recorded the data for group members that is shown in Figure 3.3.

Thus, Clients 1 and 5 had one absence, compared to three absences for Client 3, six for Client 2, and seven for Client 4.

In this example, the student defined attendance by simple presence or absence at the group. Attendance could become more complicated, for example, if some members frequently came late to group (e.g., attended for only the last 15 minutes). In such instances, the assessor must reconsider the definition of attendance. For example, a member could be counted as present if she or he was less than 15 minutes late, the construct of "minutes late" could be included as another construct in the model, or, the number of minutes the member was present during group therapy could be recorded.

COLLECT AS MUCH DATA AS POSSIBLE

Once the measurement procedure is established, the next step is to collect as much qualitative and quantitative data as possible. In general, the more information that is collected, the easier it is to interpret analyses of that information with confidence; as data are aggregated, different types of error tend to balance each other and have less of an effect (Meier, 1994). If resources permit, collect data on all process and outcome elements in the case conceptualization, and collect as much of that data as possible (e.g., in all client sessions). As described below, the quality of the data and the interpretation of the data analysis can be enhanced when the clinician makes use of continuous data collection, baseline data, and data from multiple methods.

Collect Data Continuously, Especially When Treatment Is Failing

Generally, this means that the clinician should collect information for every session or contact with the client. If the feedback loop of conceptualization, assessment, and analysis of intervention effects is to be useful, frequent, current data are needed. Continuous data collection is different from traditional expectations of gathering information only at intake and termination. Surprisingly, in a survey of 539 clinicians, Bickman and colleagues (2000) found that only 23% wanted outcome-related information more frequently than every fourth session.

Continuous data collection is also important for detecting treatment failure, particularly for measures of short-term and intermediate outcomes (Mash & Hunsley, 1993). Just as an initial conceptualization may require revision as a result of treatment failure, so may the clinician need to revise or discard initial assessment approaches. Changes in conceptualization elements means changes in construct explication and corresponding assessments and tests. And in keeping with a philosophy of expending more resources when faced with treatment failure, it may also make sense to expand data collection efforts when a client is failing. For example, instead of collecting one piece of data for an entire session (e.g., one overall rating of the client's level of affective expression), the session might be divided into multiple sections and then assessed (e.g., rate affective expression for 5-minute blocks through use of a session audiotape or observers). The use of multiple raters may also increase the validity of assessments (Hill, 1991).

Build in a Baseline Period

A *baseline* is a period of time in which outcome data are collected in the absence of an intervention (Bloom & Fischer, 1982; Hartman, 1984; Heppner et al., 1999). To the extent that resources allow, build in a baseline period with each client. For example, many clinicians traditionally employed the first two or three sessions with individual clients to obtain intake information and build rapport; if therapy is being paid by managed care companies, however, this may be unrealistic (Davis & Meier, 2001). Baseline data collected during a preintervention period can provide greater confidence that any subsequent changes that occur result from the intervention.

Figures 3.4 and 3.5 illustrate two different possible baseline periods for the case of Luke discussed in Chapter 2. The clinician used Sessions 1, 2, and 3 to gather baseline data and build a working alliance with Luke. Luke learned to self-monitor feelings of anxiety daily and then report the average daily rating for the previous week (on a scale of 1 to 10, with 10 indicating very intense anxiety). Figure 3.4 shows Luke's average anxiety ratings for the first 3 weeks of therapy. Of note in this figure is the relative stability of Luke's ratings for the three time periods of the baseline. This is the ideal situation in a baseline because if the data show an increase or decrease across the baseline, it becomes more difficult to attribute subsequent changes to the intervention alone.

In Figure 3.5, the average weekly anxiety rating, in the absence of any intervention, steadily declined during the baseline period. Even if this trend continued during the start of therapeutic interventions during Session 4, it would be difficult to attribute continued improvement to the intervention and not to other factors.

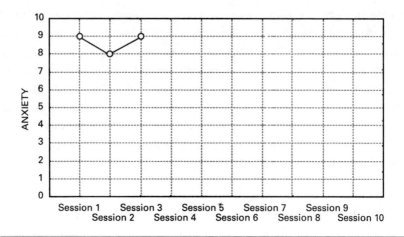

Figure 3.4   Stable Baseline Period for Luke

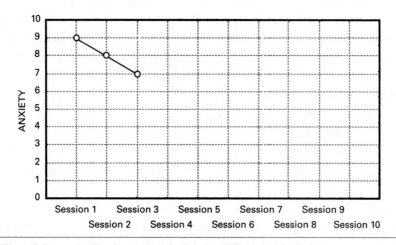

Figure 3.5   Decline in Anxiety During Baseline Period for Luke

Use Multiple Methods

The basic premise when employing multiple methods is that error introduced by any one method may be balanced by strengths in other methods
(Hartman, 1984; Paul, 1986). Thus, it might be useful for a client in treatment
for alcohol abuse to keep a record of daily alcohol consumption and to have a

second record of consumption kept by a significant other. Different data sources can be employed to corroborate each other as well as to examine if one method detected information missed by another.

As noted in the section on validity at the beginning of this chapter, every measurement method, even when applied to the same phenomenon, tends to produce different data (i.e., effects of method variance). For example, when asked to indicate the level of aggressive behavior a child exhibits at school, the child, teacher, mother, father, and classroom observer may produce significantly different estimates. Many such examples are present in the research literature. Christensen, Margolin, and Sullaway (1992) found differences between mothers' and fathers' reporting about their children ages 3 to 13 on the Child Behavior Checklist. Mothers observed more negative behaviors than did fathers, and parents disagreed about the occurrence of a behavior twice as often as they agreed. Christensen and colleagues (1992) found more consistency in descriptions of disturbed, overt, and situation-specific behaviors than in those of other kinds of behaviors. These findings, then, argue for multiple measurements of constructs and avoidance of measurement with a single method (a *mono-method bias*, in Cook & Campbell's 1979 terminology) or a single test or assessment (a *mono-operations bias*).

Use of multiple methods is particularly important in clinical settings when a reason exists to suspect that one method may be biased. For example, suppose you are the supervisor of a graduate student in her first year of training. Your supervisee, Kate, sees three to four adolescent clients in a community agency approximately every 2 weeks. As required by the agency, she completes global improvement ratings on a 100-point scale for all clients at the end of every month (lower scores indicate fewer symptoms). You have been reviewing audiotapes with Kate and discussing clients during supervision. She appears to possess adequate listening skills and, with your guidance, a basically sound approach to working with her clients. However, she also expresses considerable concern about her competence as a new clinician and how credible she appears to her clients and to you. With one of her clients, Kate has completed 12 sessions, and she now shares with you the graph of outcome data shown in Figure 3.6.

The obvious question about these ratings concerns the linear improvement of this client. Did Kate intentionally or unconsciously distort her ratings of this client's symptoms? This is a plausible explanation given that ratings of therapeutic change from clinicians are consistently higher than estimates from other sources (Lambert, 1994). While clinicians' higher estimates

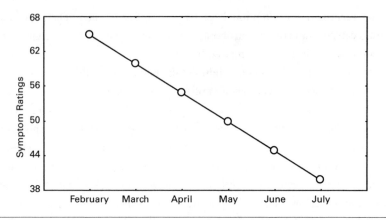

Figure 3.6   Kate's Symptom Ratings of One Client

of change may result from better observational skills as well as a bias toward seeing improvement, it is generally useful to obtain information from a second source, such as the client.

If resources allow, interpretations about treatment progress should not be made on the basis of any single measure or method. Using a variety of measures and methods (e.g., qualitative and quantitative) that follow from the case conceptualization, as well as two or more sources of information, is the fairest method for determining treatment outcomes. With multiple measures, however, it is quite likely that different measures will evidence different rates of improvement (Lambert, 1994). Halo errors should be considered when improvement occurs on all measures except in conceptualizations with a set of very general outcomes where a kind of remoralization is expected to occur (e.g., Frank & Frank, 1991; Lueger, 1998). In cases with varying outcomes, the decision to continue or end psychotherapy may then depend on such factors as the extent to which important goals have been met (particularly around target complaints) and whether resources (e.g., agency session limits, insurance reimbursement) are available to continue.

SUMMARY AND CAUTIONS

The available resources can influence decisions about the type, units, and amount of clinical measurement and assessment. Proxy measures can be an inexpensive substitute for the full construct explication and measurement of the constructs found in the case conceptualization. Situations such as treatment failure and clinical training provide a rationale for expending the resources necessary to create and employ idiographic clinical assessments. When deciding on a method of clinical assessment, however, it is also worth considering whether you have the resources necessary to *analyze* the collected data. If you plan to employ progress notes as clinical data, for example, you need to take into account that the process of qualitative analysis typically involves several readings of the text to identify and confirm important concepts. And even if you possess the requisite knowledge to conduct advanced quantitative analyses such as factor analysis, you will still need a great deal of time, as many of these techniques require hundreds of observations.

Construct validity should be the primary concern when choosing a clinical measure. Because the name of a test reflects a construct of clinical interest (e.g., The Outcome Test), do not assume that the test actually measures the named construct. In other words, face validity does not equal construct validity. The same caution applies with test *items* that appear to measure a particular phenomenon. Only evidence about construct validity can provide information about whether test scores can be usefully applied for a purpose such as measuring outcomes. Finally, in the complexity of choosing a method of clinical assessment, it is often tempting to default to a traditional measure. Such measures may be in vogue at a particular agency or seen as a standard in a particular field. I strongly encourage you to evaluate such measures independently by considering the relevant information about construct validity for your intended purpose. For example, a test that has been usefully employed for 50 years to assess psychopathology and personality characteristics may or may not be the best measure to assess therapeutic change in a particular client.

As mentioned previously, Bickman and colleagues (2000) noted that "public and private sector purchasers of mental health services see measurement of client outcomes as a form of accounting rather than as a way to improve services" (p. 72). Often the primary purpose for progress notes and outcome assessments is to provide administrative documentation rather than to influence the services provided (see American Psychological Association, 1993). For example, a clinician in private practice may keep notes to demonstrate that certain assessments and interventions were provided, whereas counseling center staff may administer symptom checklists to every client at intake and termination to demonstrate that provided services are effective. The function of assessment described in this chapter, however, is not to fulfill such legal and administrative purposes but to test and improve case conceptualizations and the interventions that flow from these formulations. The goal is to help clinicians modify, elaborate, and deepen—if not disconfirm—their initial conceptualization and treatment plans.

Much contemporary interest in assessment focuses on outcome assessment, and many observers attribute the increased attention to outcomes to the rise of managed care. However, in practice, managed care organizations (MCOs) seldom behave as if they were interested in using outcome data to improve services, rather, they employ those data for utilization review in order to constrain services (Davis & Meier, 2001). For example, Clement (1999) noted, "As I became involved with many MCOs, I was surprised by their apparent lack of interest in evaluating treatment outcomes" (pp. 91-92). Unless outcome data are fed back to the clinician in a timely and useful manner, their purpose is not improvement of clinical services.

FOUR

ANALYSES OF CLINICAL DATA

———•◦•———

Chance favors the prepared mind.
— Pasteur (cited in Kilham, 1988, p. 112)

We believe the purpose of evaluation is to inform or "enlighten"
deliberations about the value, worth, improvement, and/or future
form of services, rather than providing new knowledge, proving
cause-and-effect relationships, or producing conclusive facts.
— Speer and Newman (1996, p. 107)

Somewhere along the line in the teaching of statistics in the social
sciences, the importance of good judgment got lost amidst the
minutiae of null hypothesis testing. It is all right, indeed essential,
to argue flexibly and in detail for a particular case when you use
statistics. Data analysis should . . . make an interesting claim; it
should tell a story that an informed audience will care about, and
it should do so by intelligent interpretation of appropriate evi-
dence from empirical measurements or observations.
— Abelson (1995, p. 2)

The greatest value of a picture is when it forces us to notice what
we never expected to see.
— Tukey (1977, p. vi)

Once you have constructed a case conceptualization and collected data about its process and outcome elements, you are prepared to address clinically related questions of increasing complexity. These questions may vary by client and setting, but a common set of questions exists that can be addressed with a variety of qualitative and quantitative analytic strategies. The three major domains for these questions are

1. outcomes (i.e., client change),

2. the case conceptualization (process and outcome elements and their relationships), and

3. the assessment process (whether the measurement worked as intended).

I will address each domain in this chapter and accompany it with a description of the appropriate relevant techniques.

Approach clinical analyses in the spirit of exploration (Tukey, 1977). Do not expect analyses to provide the definitive or final answer to any question you attempt to address—too many alternative explanations are likely to be present. Given that in most clinical settings resources for anything other than direct intervention are likely to be scarce, the time available to the clinician to pursue these issues will be limited and, consequently, the answers to the questions should be considered tentative. And for reasons of resources and communicability, simple analytic methods are preferable to more complex ones.

ANALYSES RELATED TO OUTCOME

Two of the most basic questions in any clinical setting are:
    Did the client improve?
    Is the treatment working?

At first glance it may not be apparent that the answers to these two questions can be independent. Clients may improve because of factors outside of the clinical process: Situational stressors such as conflict with family members or the loss of a job may change, and so clients may become less depressed or anxious without any substantial intervention. On the other hand, some important aspects of clients' lives may deteriorate while they are in psychotherapy. Unless counseling helps to at least stabilize such clients, we may consider treatment to be failing. I discuss possible criteria for determining treatment failure later in this chapter.

Three frequently employed analytic methods for examining client improvement are time series graphs, frequency distributions, and effect size (ES).

Time Series Graphs

Time series graphs are a display of a single variable recorded over a period of time (Tufte, 1983). Time series are best employed with larger sets of data that show substantial variability or have the potential to show such variability (Tufte, 1983). Thus, time series can be very useful for examining potential changes in outcome data. Although a number of relatively complex quantitative methods exist for analyzing and interpreting time series data (e.g., conditional probability analyses, Markov models), I will focus below on what Haynes and colleagues (1993) termed a *qualitative analysis of time series.*

Many clients will evidence trends in outcome data similar to that displayed in Figure 4.1. The figure shows that the first two sessions comprise a baseline period where no intervention was present. A vertical line separates Sessions 1 and 2, the baseline period, from the intervention sessions. A client's depression scores display stability except for an increase in depressive symptoms at Sessions 3 and 6. Stability during this period is necessary if causality is to be attributed to any changes that occur during the subsequent period of intervention. Figure 4.1 displays what is known as an *A-B design* where A is the baseline and B is the intervention period. A second A-B sequence is useful to strengthen the attribution of causality to the intervention; this A-B-A-B essentially replicates the effect, showing that changes occur only during the intervention periods. The A-B-A-B design is not appropriate, however, when the change involves learning whose effects become independent of the intervention or reinforcers provided.

Depression, the outcome depicted in Figure 4.1, increases at Sessions 3 and 6. Checking process information would be useful for the clinician answering questions such as: Did a potential cause for the increase in symptoms occur at Sessions 3 and 6? It is possible that an external event (e.g., family or work stressor) occurred that resulted in an increase in depression. Although assessments of process could provide information about the variations at Sessions 3 and 6, the overall picture of outcome depicted in Figure 4.1 is of no change.

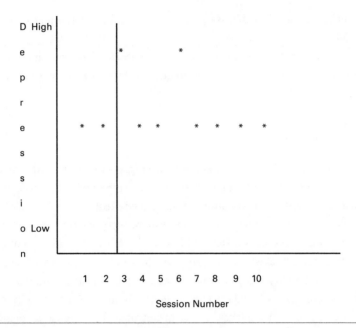

Figure 4.1   Time Series for Two Baseline Sessions and Eight Therapy Sessions

Drawing a horizontal line across the time series to represent a desired *outcome criterion level* can serve as a reminder of when treatment has been successful and termination should be discussed. In Luke's case (i.e., with presenting problems of anxiety and sleep), a discussion between Luke and the therapist during the initial sessions might lead to a decision to establish 3 (low, infrequent) as the average weekly anxiety rating Luke would like to meet to consider the therapy successful. Luke and the therapist might also agree that 3 consecutive weeks with an average rating of 3 might be sufficient to bolster Luke's confidence that the change would be subsequently maintained. Sharing and cocreating the graph with his therapist weekly might be useful feedback for Luke as well as a method for increasing his motivation (see Figure 4.2).

Small multiples (Tufte, 1983; see also Mattaini, 1993), which are particularly appropriate with two or more quantitative sets of time series data, constitute a type of graphical display that facilitates comparison of large amounts of data. Suppose, for example, that a therapist had collected quantitative information about all of the process and outcome elements in Luke's case conceptualization, as shown in Figure 4.3.

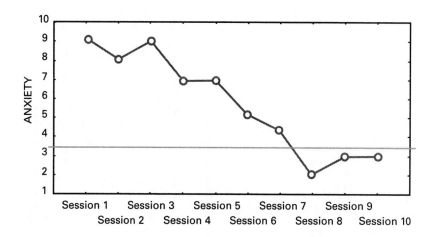

Figure 4.2 Setting a Criterion

NOTE: Luke and his therapist agreed that an average rating of 3 (indicated by the straight baseline) would indicate successful alleviation of his anxiety.

The advantage of multiples is that all of the quantitative data can be viewed at a glance. Thus, the five graphs in Figure 4.3 show that the three measures that should have decreased over time (i.e., anxiety, irrational beliefs, and sleep difficulties) did decrease. And the two measures that should have increased, the number of social interactions and the percent of eye contact made with the therapist in session, did increase. The original case conceptualization proposed for Luke in Chapter 2 suggested that Luke's social support, irrational beliefs,

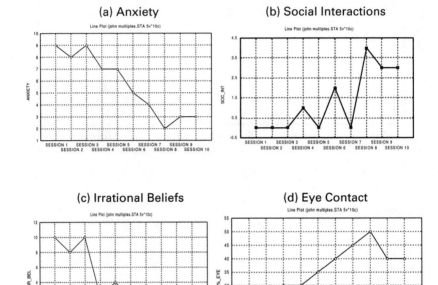

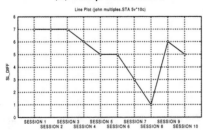

Figure 4.3   Multiple Displays of Quantitative Measures of Process and Outcome Elements in Luke's Case Conceptualization

(Continued)

(f)

Session	Anxiety Rating	Social Interactions	Irrational Beliefs	% of Eye Contact	Sleep Difficulties
1	9	0	10	20	7
2	8	0	8	25	7
3	9	0	10	30	7
4	7	1	2	30	6
5	7	0	4	35	5
6	5	2	2	40	5
7	4	0	1	45	3
8	2	4	0	50	1
9	3	3	0	40	6
10	3	3	3	40	5

NOTE: The top left graph (a) depicts his self-rated anxiety; the top right (b), the number of non-work social interactions. The middle left graph (c) shows the number of irrational beliefs spoken by Luke during the session, which were recorded by the therapist; the middle right graph (d) shows the therapist's estimate of the percentage of eye contact Luke made with the therapist during the session. The bottom left graph (e) depicts the average number of sleep difficulties Luke reported during the previous week. Plotting all of these measures on one graph would be too confusing to interpret; also, inspection of the multiples is easier than attempting to interpret the data in the accompanying table.

and social skills should be related to his anxiety and sleep problems; these graphs support those connections.

Frequency Distributions

A *frequency distribution* involves the presentation of the number of cases that have each of the attributes of a particular variable. A tally of the number of individuals who receive each possible score on a variable is a typical type of frequency distribution. Frequency distributions can be prepared either by listing the possible scores or by grouping the scores into intervals, then tallying each subject's score in the appropriate place. When all the obtained scores are entered, the tallies for each score or interval are counted to find the frequency (i.e., the number of cases for each score or interval). The sum of the frequencies will equal N, the total number of subjects.

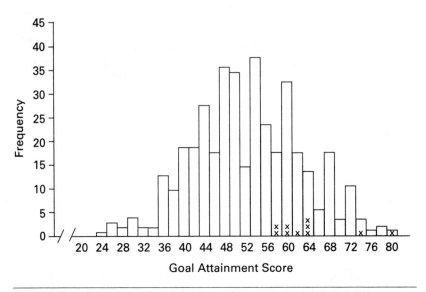

Figure 4.4   One Client's Scores in a Frequency Distribution of Scores

SOURCE: "Historical Perspective," by T. J. Kiresuk, 1994, in T. J. Kiresuk, A. Smith, & J. E. Cardillo (Eds.), *Goal Attainment Scaling: Applications, Theory, and Measurement* (pp. 135-160), Hillsdale, NJ: Lawrence Erlbaum. Copyright © 1994 by Lawrence Erlbaum. Reprinted with permission.

NOTE: The X's at the bottom of the distribution indicate the scores for all clients treated by one therapist.

Frequency distributions may be useful when comparing an individual client's score to a comparison or norm group. Kiresuk (1994), for example, indicated that community mental health staff working with Goal Attainment Scaling (GAS) methods wanted to know how well their particular clients were doing (in graph form, not statistics) in comparison to the entire group of clients at the agency. The X's in the histogram in Figure 4.4 represent one therapist's clients GAS scores within the group of scores for the whole program.

Effect Size

Clement (1999) describes a method that allows computation of an effect size for individual clients. *Effect size* (ES) is a measure of how much change results from an intervention. The advantage of Clement's use of ES, as with Kiresuk and Sherman's (1968) Goal Attainment Scaling, is that it produces a common metric that can be employed for the purposes of documentation (e.g., to demonstrate effectiveness) and local research (e.g., to investigate factors that might be related to the therapist's effectiveness, such as age of client, diagnosis, or type of treatment).

Since the seminal work of Smith and Glass (1977), ES has become the major statistical technique used in psychotherapy research to describe the amount of change resulting from an intervention. Formulas for ES are usually some variation on the following:

$$ES = \frac{\text{Mean (posttest scores)} \quad \text{Mean (pretest scores)}}{\text{Pooled Standard Deviation for posttest and pretest scores}}$$

Thus, the mean scores for a group of psychotherapy research participants on a single measure at pretest are subtracted from the mean scores for the same group at posttest; this difference score is then divided by the standard deviation of both pretest and posttest scores. The result is a standard score that can be employed as an indicator of the degree of change resulting from the intervention. Smith and Glass (1977), for example, used the ESs from a large number of studies to determine that (a) different psychotherapy approaches produced ESs of about the same size and (b) among the methodological indicators examined, ES correlated most highly with a rating of the transparency or reactivity of the outcome measures used.

Clement (1999) argued that because ES has become a standard metric, it makes sense to employ it with individual clients as well. When the focus is a single client, instead of a group as in psychotherapy research, Clement's (1999) adaptation is to have the client rate a self-generated list of problems on a 10-point scale at intake and at follow-up periods. These data are then used to compute an ES for the particular client. Clement (1999) called these Scales of Functioning (SOF) and they are completed for each client problem by the client or another person. Table 4.1 displays problems and ratings (where 10 = excellent functioning and 1 = persistent danger of hurting self or others) produced by a client.

The mean score at intake is 6.5 (standard deviation = 1.2) and at follow-up it is 7.63 (standard deviation = 1.30). Clement's (1999; Streiner, 1998) formula for computing individual ESs is:

Table 4.1   Scale of Functioning (SOF) Data of a Single Client

	1-10 Rating	
Problem Description	Intake	Follow-up
Feelings of anxiety	5	8
Feelings of depression	6	8
Anger toward deceased father	7	9
Difficulties with customers	8	9
Conflict with co-workers	7	7
Feeling manic	8	8
Feelings of self-hatred	5	7
Conflict with partner	6	5
	M = 6.5	M = 7.63
	SD = 1.2	SD = 1.30

NOTE: Higher scores indicate better functioning (see Clement, 1999).

$$ES = \frac{\text{Mean SOF (follow-up scores)} \quad \text{Mean SOF (intake scores)}}{\text{SOF Standard Deviation at Intake}}$$

So the ES for this client would be $(7.63-6.5)/1.2 = .94$. What does this number mean? Because ES has no statistical significance tests associated with it, it is difficult to know what a particular ES score means. That is, we cannot say that a particular ES is statistically significant, as we might with a correlation or the differences between the means at posttest between a treatment and control group. Instead, various researchers have proposed general guidelines for comparing ESs. Clement (1999) suggested the interpretations of ES size with individual clients shown in Table 4.2. Thus, with our hypothetical client Clement would rate the ES of .94 as improved across all problem categories.

Two cautions should be noted with Clement's approach to ES. First, all measures are weighted equally in the computation of ES. Because no one problem is the major focus of attention, the ES reflects all rated problems, regardless of their relative importance in the therapeutic process. Second, problems are selected at intake and tend to be treated as static issues from intake on; when problems are added or redefined, the assessment process must be restarted, at least for the new or redefined problem. Thus, ES may be less useful for the feedback approach described in this book than it is for administrative documentation and research purposes.

Table 4.2   Effect Size Interpretations

ES	Interpretation
1.5	Much worse
.5 to 1.49	Worse
.5 to + .5	No change
.51 to 1.49	Improved
1.5 >	Much improved

Determining Treatment Failure

As described in Chapter 2, clients frequently come to therapy with a desire to decrease negative symptoms or increase functioning and feelings of well-being (Howard, Lueger, Maling, & Martinovich, 1993). When none of these occurs, therapy can be considered a failure. Research on treatment failure can provide some criteria for determining treatment failure with individual clients.

Nierenberg and Mulroy (1997) noted that researchers in clinical trials often use a 50% improvement in symptoms as the minimal criteria to designate improvement, or they define failure as nonresponse to treatment after an intervention has been implemented for a standard period of time (e.g., no change in depression after administration of medication for 6 weeks). The time frame to consider can also depend on the theory being applied and the individual client; more severe cases require more sessions (Meier & Letsch, 2000). Dose-response studies of the effects of psychotherapy on improvement provide no absolute guidelines for when improvement should begin to occur. Howard, Kopta, Krause, and Orlinsky (1986), for example, found that 50% of clients in 15 outcome studies evidenced improvement by the eighth session, whereas Kadera, Lambert, and Andrews's (1996) study found a longer interval necessary for improvement in their client sample. Given that research suggests that many clients evidence improvement during initial sessions (Kopta, Howard, Lowry, & Beutler, 1994; Sperry, Brill, Howard, & Grissom, 1996), a general rule of thumb is that a client who does not evidence improvement within 10 to 20 sessions should be tentatively considered a treatment failure. The major purpose of such a declaration, of course, is that alternative plans should be considered.

One nomothetic strategy to decide whether therapy is successful involves determining if clients fall within a range of functional scores on an

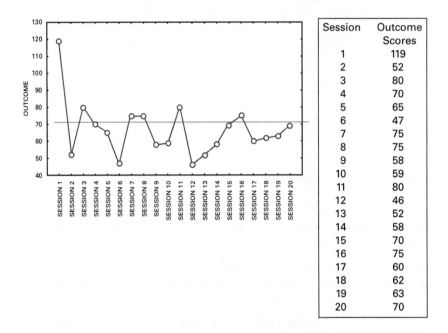

Session	Outcome Scores
1	119
2	52
3	80
4	70
5	65
6	47
7	75
8	75
9	58
10	59
11	80
12	46
13	52
14	58
15	70
16	75
17	60
18	62
19	63
20	70

Figure 4.5   Quantitative Criterion for Successful Completion of Therapy

outcome measure such as the OQ-45. Functional in this sense means scores obtained by a community or nonclinical sample on the scale (see e.g., Kadera et al., 1996). In Kadera and colleagues' study, a score of 66 or less on the OQ-45 was necessary to move from the dysfunctional range to the functional scores. A major problem with these type of normative approaches involves clients who fall into and out of such criteria in a short period, as Figure 4.5 illustrates.

Because this client's scores do not stabilize below the criterion score of 66, making decisions about treatment success is difficult. (See Kadera and colleagues, 1996, for similar examples.) Managed care companies, however, may terminate authorization for therapy the first time a client meets a quantitative criterion (see Davis & Meier, 2001). In general, interpreting the results of an analysis of clinical data to detect treatment failure should depend on theoretical expectations in the context of the individual case.

ANALYSES RELATED TO CONCEPTUALIZATION

Particularly if the client is not improving or if the treatment is not working, another set of questions becomes important:

Why did the client worsen?

Is the client conceptualization sufficient to explain changes in the client's behavior?

Is the client conceptualization useful in planning the intervention or interventions?

As with questions about outcome, a variety of methods can be usefully employed to address conceptualization issues. The use of qualitative analysis, tables, graphic displays, scatterplots and correlations, descriptive statistics, time series, and combining qualitative and quantitative analyses are described below.

Qualitative Analysis of Progress Notes

Table 4.3 contains an initial extraction of important themes, summarized in one or two sentences per session, that emerged from qualitative analysis of progress notes from individual therapy with a depressed client (Meier, 1999). This information contains potentially important themes for the elements of a case conceptualization. For example, the client's ideas about his role in the conflicted relationships of his family of origin and his continuing efforts to create a new family life appear to be important process elements. His tendency to avoid processing intense emotional material (and the resulting pace at which the therapist could effectively introduce this material) may also be important for conceptualizing potential interventions.

The focus of qualitative research is the identification of important con-structs, themes, and narratives contained in interviews or text (Creswell, 1994; Strauss & Corbin, 1997). In a clinical context, qualitative analysis of progress notes is a particularly useful method for identifying information related to process and outcome elements in a case conceptualization.

Although a variety of methods exist for qualitative analysis, many approaches share a common technique of rereading original material to perform careful comparisons, detect differences, note patterns, and see trends (Miles &

Table 4.3   Qualitative Analysis of Progress Notes With an Individual Client

Session	Key Issues
1	Presenting problem centers on depression and anxiety; agrees to referral for possible medication; reports history of conflicted family relationships, particularly with long-deceased alcoholic father
2	Has started medication and will continue counseling; reports difficulty at work with "crazy" customers; we establish a schedule of activities designed to increase positive reinforcement for him
3	Reports a history of trying to recreate a family life with people other than immediate family of origin; for example, becomes a physical, emotional caretaker for distant relatives, older neighbors; reports no effect from reinforcement activities
4	Reports that he is very angry with many past incidents with family of origin, particularly father, and some current events with mother
5	Much less anxious, moderately less depressed, but seems almost manic; very strong emotional reactions to many current events
6	Agrees to start a journal where he writes thoughts, feelings, and related events
7	Reports that he has come to the conclusion that he hates himself; reads books about identity development; now has frequent arguments with partner
8	Reports becoming easily angry with co-workers, even when their behavior does not affect him directly, as well as with partner and family members
9	Reads for 30 minutes from a journal about past family incidents that provoked anger, rage, and sadness in him; question arises whether he should pursue family therapy with mother and siblings
10	Notes that he is angry with his mother but cannot express those feelings to her or even explore much in session; family culture indicates that being angry with parents is equivalent to disobeying them
11	Despite his father's death 15 years ago, reports that he still wishes there was some way he could be emotionally close to father; I confront him about this unrealistic idea; he later cancels next session
12	Some processing in session of how he experiences emotion; relates stories that provide evidence (to him) that his role was to function as emotional caretaker in his family; tried to protect mother from abusive, alcoholic father
13	No-show; later reports that he forgot about the session

Table 4.3 *(Continued)*

14	Wonders whether to stay in current relationship; debates financial security versus partner's treating him like a child
15	Considers whether to leave town, start a new life elsewhere; now spends much time considering therapy issues between sessions
16	Same issues as Session 15
17	Ran into his brother's friend who had no idea that client's father was alcoholic; confirms for client that mother and siblings denied family difficulties; I note that in the past he denied such problems as well
18	Clearly has changed locus of responsibility for family conflict away from himself; his anger and rumination about family has decreased; focuses more on work, other people
19	Discusses buying a house with partner; one brother is now contacting him for social interactions
20	Termination; client reports greater self-confidence, emotional independence from family, stable work performance; describes himself as "better integrated"

SOURCE: Meier (1999).

Huberman, 1990). In a *grounded theory analysis* (Creswell, 2002; Strauss & Corbin, 1997), the method involves explicit identification of important concepts in fieldnotes (i.e., grounding the theory in the fieldnotes). This material is then subjected to a coding scheme designed to organize it conceptually (Strauss & Corbin, 1997). In the grounded theory method, the analyst generates theoretical constructs that explain the actions and processes occurring in a social setting. Grounded theory takes a constructivist perspective, assuming that individuals filter their versions of reality through the meaning they attribute to situations.

Important information related to outcome is also present in Table 4.3. Suppose, for example, that the clinician working with this client was employing a *common factors approach,* in which a variety of positive effects are expected to occur (Frank & Frank, 1991). The clinician could employ the qualitative explication of the construct of outcome in Figure 4.6 in preparation for a qualitative analysis of the progress notes in Table 4.3.

Based on this explication, the clinician could reexamine the progress note extracts in Table 4.3 to determine the themes that are related to the outcome effects (in bold type in Table 4.4).

Construct: *Outcome Effects*

General definition:

Intermediate and long-term positive and negative effects resulting from therapy

Elaboration that describes critical parts of behavior:

Outcomes indicated by client reports and clinician observations regarding affect, behavior, cognitions related to changes in client presenting and emerging problems

Typical examples:

Less anxiety, decisions about work options are examples of outcomes

Questionable instances:

Outcomes donít include other incidental reports of changes in behavior, affect, cognition

Figure 4.6   Qualitative Explication of Outcome

The relevant outcome information in bold type in Table 4.4 includes:

1. In Session 5, his anxiety is reported to have lessened considerably, while his depression lessened moderately.

2. In Sessions 14, 15, and 16, he is contemplating significant changes in his primary relationship, work, and living arrangements.

3. In Session 18, he reports less guilt about his role in family conflict and less worrying and anger about his family.

4. And finally, in Session 20, he concludes therapy by reporting greater self-confidence, emotional independence, and stable work performance.

Tables

A major consideration during and after the process of qualitative analysis concerns how to display the information. *Tables* are a common method. Although how information is ordered in a table depends on the particular situation, Henry (1995) recommended that rows and columns be ordered so that the most interesting information is presented first. Tables can also be used

Table 4.4   Qualitative Analysis of Progress Notes With an Individual Client

Session	Key Issues
1	Presenting problem centers on depression and anxiety; agrees to referral for possible medication; reports history of conflicted family relationships, particularly with long-deceased alcoholic father
2	Has started medication and will continue counseling; reports difficulty at work with "crazy" customers; we establish a schedule of activities designed to increase positive reinforcement for him
3	Reports a history of trying to recreate a family life with people other than immediate family of origin; for example, becomes a physical, emotional caretaker for distant relatives, older neighbors; reports no effect from reinforcement activities
4	Reports that he is very angry with many past incidents with family of origin, particularly father, and some current events with mother
5	**Much less anxious, moderately less depressed, but seems almost manic**; very strong emotional reactions to many current events
6	Agrees to start a journal where he writes thoughts, feelings, and related events
7	Reports that he has come to the conclusion that he hates himself; reads books about identity development; now has frequent arguments with partner
8	Reports becoming easily angry with co-workers, even when their behavior does not affect him directly, as well as with partner and family members
9	Reads for 30 minutes from a journal about past family incidents that provoked anger, rage, and sadness in him; question arises whether he should pursue family therapy with mother and siblings
10	Notes that he is angry with his mother but cannot express those feelings to her or even explore much in session; family culture indicates that being angry with parents is equivalent to disobeying them
11	Despite his father's death 15 years ago, reports that he still wishes there was some way he could be emotionally close to father; I confront him about this unrealistic idea; he later cancels next session
12	Some processing in session of how he experiences emotion; relates stories that provide evidence (to him) that his role was to function as emotional caretaker in his family; tried to protect mother from abusive, alcoholic father
13	No-show; later reports that he forgot about the session

(Continued)

Table 4.4 *(Continued)*

14	**Wonders whether to stay in current relationship**; debates financial security versus partner's treating him like a child
15	**Considers whether to leave town**, start a new life elsewhere; now spends much time considering therapy issues between sessions
16	Same issues as Session 15
17	Ran into his brother's friend who had no idea that client's father was alcoholic; confirms for client that mother and siblings denied family difficulties; I note that in the past he denied such problems as well
18	**Clearly has changed locus of responsibility for family conflict, moved it away from himself; his anger and rumination about family has decreased**; focuses more on work, other people
19	Discusses buying a house with partner; one brother is now contacting him for social interactions
20	**Termination; client reports greater self-confidence, emotional independence from family, stable work performance; describes himself as "better integrated"**

SOURCE: Meier (1999).

NOTE: Bold type indicates material relevant to outcome.

to present quantitative information, and some research indicates that it is easier for many people to extract information correctly from a table than from a graph (Henry, 1995). Miles and Huberman (1994) indicated that two major types of qualitative data displays exist: matrices and networks. A *matrix* consists of rows and columns of information where two lists of qualitative information are crossed. Tables 4.3 and 4.4 represent a rudimentary matrix where session number (time) is crossed by session themes. *Networks* are qualitative concepts or nodes with links illustrating relationships between the nodes. Feedback loops, such as the process-outcome models displayed in this book, are one illustration of a network. As with all analytic methods, qualitative displays should be designed to facilitate exploration of data and illustrate key concepts.

In addition to presenting qualitative information, as done earlier in this chapter, tables can also be employed to display presence/absence data. Recall the example from Chapter 3 of the student clinician who posited a positive relation between group attendance and an absence of drug use. Table 4.5 contains data about attendance and drug use (as confirmed by urinalysis),

Table 4.5   Attendance and Drug Use in a Substance Abuse Group

Session	Client Attendance					Drug Use				
	C^1	C^2	C^3	C^4	C^5	C^1	C^2	C^3	C^4	C^5
1		A		A		P	P			P
2				A		P				
3		A		A		P				
4		A		A		P				P
5		A	A			P				
6	A	A	A	A		P				
7		A	A	A		P				
8				A	A	P				

NOTE: "C" stands for client; "A" indicates that the client was absent for that session; "P" indicates that a urinalysis indicated that drugs were present.

which are factors potentially reflecting an important process (attendance)-outcome (drug use) relation.

At the level of individual clients, there appears to be an imperfect relation between attendance and presence of drugs. Client 2's frequent absences are associated with the presence of drugs, while Client 4's are not. In fact, the model would seem to be consistent only in the case of Client 2. Clearly, factors in addition to or other than attendance are influencing drug use among most group members.

We can employ these data to evaluate treatment success and failure as well. If total abstinence was the goal of the group, Clients 1, 3, 4, and 5 have succeeded by Session 5. For Client 2, the question remains, what influenced abstinence? Attendance may be related to Client 2's abstinence, but other, intermediate constructs apparently need to be addressed first.

Graphic Displays

Graphs and other images have a variety of analytic purposes (Tufte, 1983), such as (a) helping the viewer to think about the substance of results rather than the methodology or display characteristics; (b) revealing data at several levels of detail, from a broad overview to fine structure; and (c) aiding in the retention of important information. Graphics can be employed as a tool for reasoning about the qualitative and quantitative assessment data collected on the basis of case conceptualizations (see Howard et al., 1996).

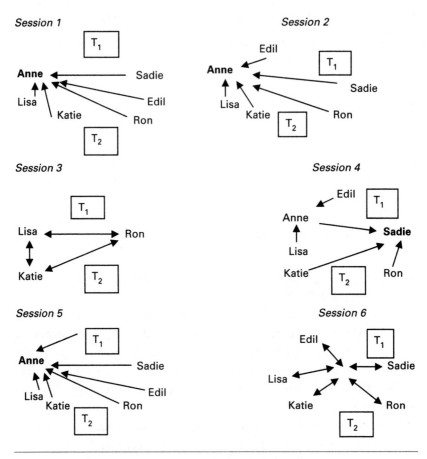

Figure 4.7   Graphic Representation of a Psychotherapy Group's Process

NOTE: This figure was reconstructed from hand-drawn notes of psychotherapy process for a group. Group members are designated by their names; their locations in the diagram show their approximate seating locations. T_1 and T_2 refer to the group's co-leaders. Arrows show the most frequent directions of conversation and attention in the group. Lines with single arrows indicate that the focus is on that person; lines with double arrows indicate a feedback loop between group members. Anne monopolizes most group sessions until a co-leader intervenes with her in Session 5.

Figure 4.7 contains a graphic of a psychotherapy group's process that is a network display of qualitative information. As illustrated, Anne monopolized Sessions 1 and 2. Anne is not present in Session 3, and the result is greater group interaction and cohesion. Sadie takes on more of the monopolizer role in Session 4, but in Session 5 Anne reclaims that role. In Session 5, a co-leader intervenes with Anne about her monopolizing; Anne responds by dropping out. The result in Session 6 is that the remaining members begin to pay attention to process and affect—the signs of a cohesive experiential group (see Yalom, 1995).

As the process in the figure illustrates, perhaps the single most important act group leaders can perform before their group begins is to screen members. *Screening* permits the development of a relatively homogeneous group, thereby facilitating modeling and cohesion (Yalom, 1995). In the group illustrated in Figure 4.7, the leaders were unable to prescreen their members and thus had no knowledge of the members' ability to interact appropriately in the group. The result was the presence of a group member (Anne) who monopolized the group's attention and prevented the other members from developing into a cohesive group. Yalom (1995) suggests that the following individuals be excluded from groups: (a) persons who experience difficulty relating to others (e.g., those with diagnoses such as schizophrenia), (b) persons who cannot attend the group regularly (e.g., missing even one of every five sessions), and (c) persons with acute situational crises. Persons in crisis may be considerably less interested in the group when their situation changes, and research suggests that the best outcomes occur for persons who are experiencing moderate discomfort (Yalom, 1995).

Another variation on qualitative analysis of progress notes involves graphic displays of process-outcome elements by session. Consider a career counseling case described by Kirschner, Hoffman, and Hill (1994). Janet, a 43-year-old divorced White woman with two children, volunteered to participate in a study examining process and outcome elements in career counseling. Kirschner and colleagues described Janet as a speech therapist with 8 years of experience in a public school system who was dissatisfied with her current job, unsure why she was dissatisfied, and unsure of her vocational interests and skills. Janet listed three goals for the career counseling: (a) to discover career areas that matched her skills and interests, (b) to make new contacts with persons in career-related fields, and (c) to decide whether to stay in the school system or leave it. These process and outcome elements are listed in the first model box in Figure 4.8.

Janet met with a psychologist for seven 50-minute sessions. Following an intake session and a session interpreting the results of a vocational interest inventory, subsequent sessions focused on assessment of work values, skills, and interests; learning how to research occupational information; and discussion of Janet's self-efficacy expectations, career identity, and self-worth. Outside the sessions, Janet found information about different career areas, listed

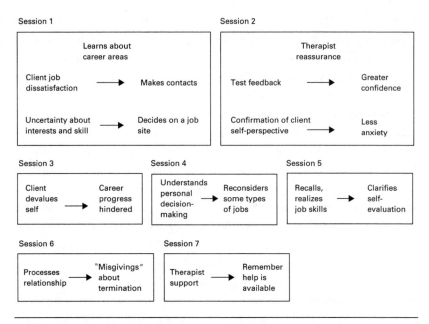

Figure 4.8   Changing Process-Outcome Elements Over Seven Sessions of Career Counseling With Janet

NOTE: See Kirschner et al. (1994) for more information.

potential careers, contacted individuals about career possibilities, and listed the advantages and disadvantages of alternate job sites. Kirschner and colleagues (1994, p. 222, Table 5) described the process and outcome data by session that are displayed graphically in the boxes in Figure 4.8. Although many of these elements are common to career counseling (e.g., the test feedback in Session 2), others are atypical but were potentially useful for working with Janet in career counseling (e.g., reconsidering some types of jobs after understanding her decision-making style in Session 4; processing her ambivalence about termination in Session 6). Thus, adding new elements and modifying initial elements were important to understanding the clinical process as sessions progressed with Janet, and displaying them in graphic boxes provides an easily accessible reminder of those key insights and critical incidents.

The usefulness of graphics depends on both the skills of the graph creator and the graph's audience. Henry (1995) noted that the graph maker's competence depends on his or her knowledge of the subject, choice of meaningful data, and ability to tailor display designs. The choice of meaningful data is particularly important: As Tufte (1990, p. 34) noted, "If the numbers are boring, then you've got the wrong numbers." This aphorism obviously applies to qualitative information as well. The role of the audience includes its motivation to know the presented material, ability to interpret the display (which may depend on familiarity with particular types of graphs), and knowledge of the subject (Henry, 1995).

Scatterplots and Correlations

A *scatterplot* is a graphical representation of the relation between quantitative measures of two constructs. Examination of a scatterplot indicates the strength and direction of that relation. A *correlation* is the numeric summary of the extent to which two constructs covary.

Scatterplots and correlations can be employed to examine the degree of covariation between elements in a case conceptualization. Such covariation is a prerequisite for causality: Without correlation between two constructs presumed to be linearly related, no causality is possible. A scatterplot's advantage over correlation is that a scatterplot can provide a visual picture of nonlinear relations, whereas correlation is chiefly an index of the strength of a linear relation between two variables.

For example, suppose your client's presenting problem is shyness. Much of the clinical work might focus on the client's taking such interpersonal risks as initiating conversations with friends and strangers, inviting friends to lunch and social events, and responding positively to invitations from others. The client's homework assignment is to take such risks and record the number of risks taken and the number of positive interactions with others. Figure 4.9 displays a scatterplot of the number of risks and positive interactions per week reported by the client over 10 sessions.

Correlations can range from 1.00 to 1.00, and this scatterplot (showing relations between symptoms and time) evidences a correlation of .93. That is, as the client took more risks, this was strongly related to an increase in positive social interactions.

A second example concerns a novice clinician who feared he was asking too many questions with a particular client, thereby inhibiting the client's exploration of feelings. Figure 4.10 displays a summary of the data he collected about the relation between the number of questions he asked and the number of feeling words spoken by a client during the same session.

The plot provides evidence that clinician questions are negatively associated with the client's expression of affect. That is, as the number of clinician questions increases, the client's use of affective expressions decreases. The

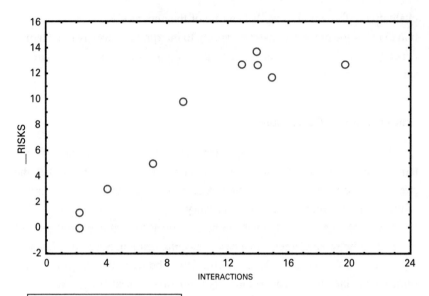

Number of Positive Social Interactions	Number of Risks Taken
2	0
2	1
4	3
7	5
9	10
15	12
14	13
20	13
13	13
14	14

Figure 4.9   Scatterplot of Client's Number of Risks Taken and Number of
Positive Social Interactions

NOTE: The relationship between these two measures is positive (as one construct increases, so does the other) and linear (with one exception, the points can be arranged along a line).

actual correlation computed for the six pairs of data displayed adjacent to the scatterplot is .88. Although other explanations can account for the association between greater client feeling words and fewer clinician questions, such data can provide the impetus for students to monitor and regulate their behaviors in session.

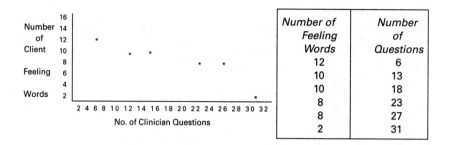

Figure 4.10 Relation Between Clinician Questions and Client Affective Expression

Table 4.6 Correlation Coefficients for Luke's Process and Outcome Data

Measures	*2*	*3*	*4*	*5*
Process Constructs				
1. Social Interactions	.67	.68	.84	.75
2. Irrational Beliefs		.84	.87	.70
3. Percentage of Eye Contact			.91	.88
Outcome Constructs				
4. Anxiety				.76
5. Sleep Difficulties				

Recall that Luke's case conceptualization (in Chapter 2) suggested that Luke's social support, irrational beliefs, and social skills should be related to his anxiety and sleep problems. Data for these constructs were presented in Figure 4.3. As shown in Table 4.6, more specific relations can be examined if correlation coefficients are computed for these data.

The correlations indicate that process constructs correlate in expected directions (e.g., the number of social interactions is negatively correlated with irrational beliefs, $r = .67$) as do outcome constructs (e.g., anxiety and sleep difficulties are positively correlated). Process and outcome constructs correlate among themselves in expected directions, and the particularly high correlations between percentage of eye contact and both outcome constructs suggest that this measure of social skills may be particularly worthy of further attention.

Session	Number of Feeling Words	Number of Questions
1	12	6
2	10	13
3	10	18
4	8	23
5	8	27
6	2	31

Number of Feeling Words	
Mean:	8.33
Median:	9
Standard Deviation:	3.44
Range:	10
Number of Questions	
Mean:	19.67
Median:	20.5
Standard Deviation:	9.24
Range:	25

Figure 4.11   Descriptive Statistics for Two Measures by Session

Descriptive Statistics

These are procedures for describing, summarizing, and organizing quantitative information. Descriptive statistics are usually contrasted with *inferential statistics*, which are procedures for making inferences about a population based on a sample drawn from that population (Vogt, 1999). Statistical procedures may be seen as more rigorous than graphics for confirming hypotheses (see O'Neill, 1993). Paul (1987a) noted that descriptive statistics can be useful for examining absolute levels of scores; for examining scores in relation to identified events, in relation to local groups, and in comparison with regional and local norms; and for comparing scores at different times. Descriptive statistics likely to be of use in clinical settings include *measures of central tendency, range, standard deviation*, and detection of *outliers*. These are simple statistical procedures that can be computed with or without statistical analysis software.

To illustrate these statistics, recall the earlier example of the student clinician who wished to examine the relation between the number of questions he asked in session and the number of affective words used by his client. The subsequent data were shown in Figure 4.10 and are reproduced in Figure 4.11 along with accompanying descriptive statistics.

Measures of central tendency are numeric estimates of the middle values of a frequency distribution of scores. Calculate the *mean* (i.e., average) by taking the sum of the scores in a group and dividing the number of scores. The *median* is the middle score when all the scores have been arranged in order of size; 50% of the scores in a group are above the median and 50% are below. Finally, the *mode* is simply the most frequently occurring score; this can be a useful statistic with a large set of data.

Two statistics intended to describe the spread of scores in a frequency distribution are the range and the standard deviation. The *range* is simply the total spread of scores in a distribution, found by subtracting the smallest number from the largest. The *standard deviation* (SD) is the square root of the variance of a group of scores, a measure of variability that indicates the degree to which a group of scores disperse about the mean. The standard deviation is the average deviation of scores from the mean; the larger the standard deviation, the more widely spread the distribution of scores.

An *outlier* is an extreme value in a set of data and can be useful for identifying unusual events or circumstances and detecting errors in data entry. In a statistical sense, outliers are important because they can distort the interpretation of data and cause summary statistics to be misleading. If a set of data contains an outlier, for example, the mean is likely to be skewed toward the outlier; thus, the mean will not be a good indication of the center of the distribution of scores. In a normally distributed set of data, values of the mean and median will be similar.

Returning to the data in Figure 4.10, note that the mean and median for feeling words (8.33 and 9, respectively) and number of questions (19.67, 20.5) are similar, suggesting that few or no outliers are present. If outliers are part of a set of data, they can be trimmed (i.e., eliminated) if the purpose of descriptive statistics about that set is to summarize the scores. For clinical feedback purposes, however, outliers are often important because they can suggest that an unusual process or event has occurred. Also, the values of the standard deviation and range for both measures in Figure 4.11 indicate that there is considerable variation in this set of data; variation is important, for example, if you wish to detect change over time or avoid attenuation in correlations.

In a clinical context, descriptive statistics can also be usefully interpreted by comparison with each other. A simple *line plot* (Tukey, 1977) can be a starting point for exploration and reasoning about the data. Figure 4.12 shows such a plot for the number of client feeling words from the previous example.

As shown in this Figure, all but 2 of these values are within 1 standard deviation of the mean. The value of "2" feeling words (Case 6 in Figure 4.12) is well outside the 1 standard deviation level, suggesting that something

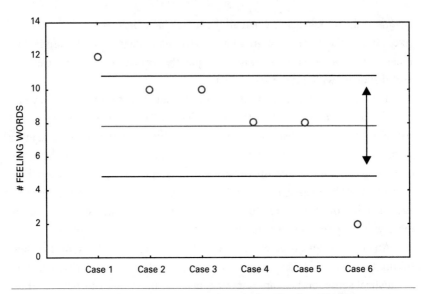

Figure 4.12   Plot of Values for the Number of Client Feeling Words

NOTE: In this line plot of the values for this construct, the middle line indicates the mean for the values while the lines above and below indicate 1 standard deviation.

unusual is happening in this case. As shown in Figure 4.9, the client uttered only 2 feeling words when the student clinician asked his greatest number of questions, 31. Also, the plot makes clear that most of the values are in the 8 to 10 range, suggesting a plateau for the number of feeling words this client will express during any session.

Time Series

The data contained in a time series can also provide information relevant to a case conceptualization. Suppose, for example, that Luke's anxiety worsened toward the end of therapy. Clinical work with Luke quickly led to decreases in anxiety ratings over Sessions 3 to 8 (Figure 4.13). After Session 8, however, the clinician discussed Luke's progress with the managed care company's utilization reviewer; the reviewer believed that significant progress had been made and decided to authorize only three more sessions. The therapist communicated the decision to Luke during the beginning of Session 9, and Luke agreed to terminate after Session 12. At the end of Session 9, however,

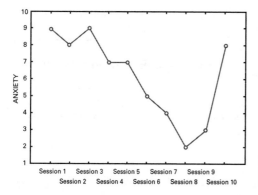

Session	Anxiety Rating
1	9
2	8
3	9
4	7
5	7
6	5
7	4
8	2
9	3
10	8

Figure 4.13   Luke's Anxiety Ratings Over 10 Sessions of Psychotherapy

NOTE: With Luke's ratings, higher numbers indicated greater anxiety.

he began to express ambivalence about ending therapy. When Luke arrived for Session 10, he shared his anxiety ratings for the previous week (Figure 4.13), which had rebounded back to 8. Although the clinician reviewed the strategies that Luke had successfully been employing at work and home, Luke alternately appeared reassured and doubtful about whether these strategies would work when he tried them by himself after the conclusion of therapy.

The data at Session 9 indicate that some threshold has been crossed, and the initial intake information and case conceptualization may offer clues as to why Luke's anxiety rebounded. If the therapist became Luke's sole source of social support, and if Luke developed no other social connections during the course of therapy, he may be very reluctant to leave the therapist. In addition, the clinical literature includes some theory that predicts that many clients, even at the conclusion of successful therapy, will resist termination of treatment (see, e.g., Teyber, 2000). From the perspective of psychodynamic and attachment theories, ending therapy can become a separation experience that must be dealt with as a therapeutic issue in and of itself. With this second explanation the conceptualization can be revised as shown in Figure 4.14.

If Luke made no additional social connections during therapy, the anticipated loss of the therapeutic relationship would likely be further magnified. Based on this reconceptualization, it would be wise to assess how important

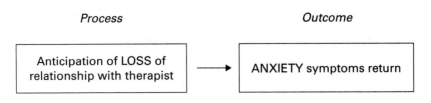

Figure 4.14   New Process and Outcome Elements in Luke's Conceptualization

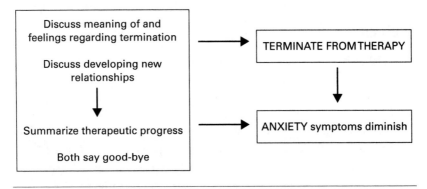

Figure 4.15   A Revised Conceptualization for Luke

the clinical relationship is for Luke and consider how to deal with termination as a therapeutic task. For example, we might propose the model shown in Figure 4.15.

Thus, the new focus of therapy would be a proper termination. If this conceptualization was useful and successfully implemented, Luke's anxiety would diminish, closure would be placed on therapy, and Luke's attention would turn to developing new social relationships. Although other therapeutic strategies might be successful, this conceptualization presents one approach for interpreting Luke's behavior and for considering what to do as well as what not to do (e.g., refer Luke to another therapist for long-term therapy).

Another useful variation of time series graphs that can inform conceptualization involves tracking session themes over time. Each client typically presents with multiple problems; each client usually discusses multiple problems within each session. Although the conceptualization approach in this book

Table 4.7 Client Themes by Session

	Session							
Theme	*1*	*2*	*3*	*4*	*5*	*6*	*7*	*8*
Anxiety	X	X	X	X	X	X	X	
Family Issues	X							
Finances	X	X						
Lack of Friends								
Emotional Independence		X		X	X	X	X	X
Termination							X	X

emphasizes the selection of a smaller subset of problems, it can be informative to track themes discussed within session, over time, as shown in Table 4.7.

If the client themes depicted in Table 4.7 belonged to Luke, this might suggest that emotional independence was a more significant element than the clinician initially thought it was. In general, secondary themes that a client consistently brings up in therapy deserve additional consideration in the conceptualization. Finally, note that this type of analysis might be most usefully employed after an initial qualitative analysis of progress notes (as described earlier in this chapter) identifies the major themes addressed in therapy.

Combining Qualitative and Quantitative Analyses

In general, the combination of qualitative and quantitative information in the same display provides richer information for analysis and interpretation of information related to process and outcome elements and relationships. Gottman and Leiblum (1974), for example, noted that a brief description of critical incidents can be attached to a time series to provide possible explanations for changes in data. As shown in Figure 4.16, this can be particularly helpful for noticing and remembering recurring events in a client's life. The death of this client's father and the anniversary of that death are associated with two of the highest levels of depression for this client.

As shown in Figure 4.17, Corcoran and Gingerich (1994) created another method of combining qualitative and quantitative information on the same page. The advantage here is that all relevant data are easily accessible for review or presentation to other persons. One potential disadvantage lies in the fact that in trying to place all relevant data in one page, some important information may be lost.

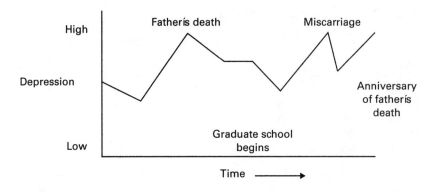

Figure 4.16   Relationship of Depression and Critical Incidents in a Client's Life

NOTE: The therapist could explore these events to learn how they influence the client's levels of depression (see Gottman & Leiblum, 1974). See the example of Tsui-Ling in Chapter 5.

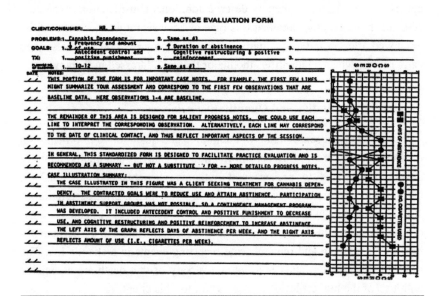

Figure 4.17   Combining Qualitative and Quantitative Data in a Progress Record

SOURCE: "Practice Evaluation in the Context of Managed Care: Case-Recording Methods for Quality Assurance Reviews," by K. Corcoran and W. J. Gingerich, 1994, *Research on Social Work Practice*, 4, pp. 326-337. Copyright 1994 by Sage Publications. Reprinted with permission.

One question on a survey of seventh and eighth grade students asked them to report the types of bullying-related problems they had observed occurring to themselves or others. The plot displays the percentage of students who observed the activities listed during the previous school year. Figure 4.18 displays their results along with a text box that provided additional information.

The most frequently observed behaviors were students using offensive language (reported by 90% of the students), students physically fighting one another (reported by 87%), students verbally threatening one another (reported by 87%), and bullying (reported by 80%). As noted in the text, the number of bullying incidents observed appeared related to the presence or absence of a father or stepfather in the home. Whether the client is a group, as in this example, or an individual, the combination of qualitative and quantitative information provides a richer source of information for conceptualization and interpretation of results than would either type of information alone.

ANALYSES RELATED TO ASSESSMENT

Several of the analytic approaches described earlier in this chapter can also be employed to examine assessment problems. Such problems include situations where clinical work is successful but the outcome measures employed do not reflect the changes that are occurring. In addition, data from different sources (e.g., therapist, client, teacher, employer) may vary in their estimates of the direction and amount of client change. If there are problems in the process of answering questions about client change or understanding client behavior, relevant inquiries include:

What evidence is there that the measurements of client and counseling constructs are reliable and valid for their intended purposes?

What factors besides the intended constructs might be influencing scores on these measurements?

Using Multiple Time Series to Estimate Validity

Recall from Chapter 3 that validity refers to the inferences for which a test's scores can be employed. One way to investigate the validity of a

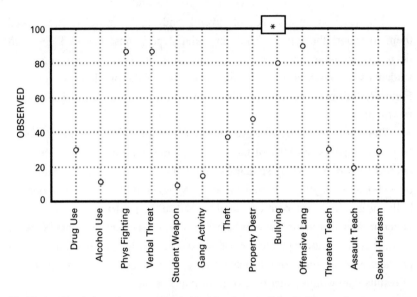

*Students with a father at home reported observing fewer bullying incidents, whereas students with a stepfather at home reported observing more bullying incidents.

Problem	% of Students Who Observed Problem
Drug Use	30
Alcohol Use	11
Physical Fighting	87
Verbal Threats	87
Student Weapon	9
Gang Activity	15
Theft	37
Property Destruction	48
Bullying	80
Offensive Language	90
Threaten Teacher	30
Assault Teacher	20
Sexual Harassment	29

Figure 4.18   Combining a Time Series With a Text Box

NOTE: This display summarizes the percentage of students who observed these problems at school. The text supplements the quantitative displays with further information about one category, bullying.

measure is to compare it with a second measure intended to measure the same construct for the same purpose (i.e., convergent validity). Suppose, for example, you work with a college student who presents with depression and a social phobia that sometimes prevents her from attending classes. Your client model indicates that the social phobia is causing the depression and the missed classes. You instruct the client to self-monitor the number of classes she misses; as part of normal counseling center data collection, she also completes a Beck Depression Inventory-2 at intake, termination, and at least one midpoint. As shown in Figure 4.19, the graph presents both the number of classes she misses (values multiplied by 2, with circles) and her BDI-2 scores (in boxes).

As shown in the figure, the number of classes missed by the client decreased steadily with time, while her BDI-2 scores slightly increased. These client data suggest that the client changed her attendance behavior, but it did not influence her depression. Why did the client's BDI-2 scores remains stable? Among the possible explanations is that the BDI was invalid for measuring depression with this client, in this clinical situation. For example, the interventions may have been behavioral in nature and designed to change such behaviors as class attendance first. Changes in depressive cognition and affect might eventually follow the behavioral changes (recall the discussion in Chapter 3 of desynchrony).

Also noteworthy in this example is that some data are missing for both outcome measures, a common situation in clinical settings. Extrapolation from clinical data sets with missing data may often be necessary; it should be done cautiously, however, particularly as the amount of missing data increases.

Using Correlations to Estimate Validity

With one of my individual clients, I was concerned with how he was experiencing and expressing affect in session. Several potential indicators of affective experience and expression were apparent with this client, and I was uncertain which might serve as the best proxy measure. Consequently, at the end of each session I rated four constructs on a 1 to 5 (low to high) scale:

1. how much helplessness he expressed in session (e.g., "I can't handle anything in my life");

2. how aware he was of his feelings (e.g., he expressed considerable helplessness but seemed unaware of other feelings, such as anger and sadness);

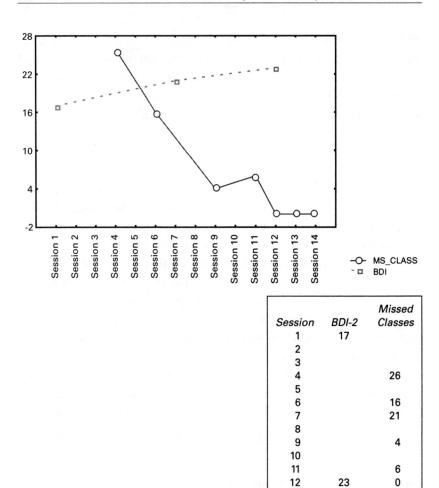

Session	BDI-2	Missed Classes
1	17	
2		
3		
4		26
5		
6		16
7		21
8		
9		4
10		
11		6
12	23	0
13		0
14		0

Figure 4.19   Time Series of Missed Classes and BDI Scores

NOTE: The circles indicate the number of classes the client missed in the previous week (divide by 2 for the actual number); the boxes are her BDI-2 scores. Data are missing for the number of missed classes for Sessions 5, 7, 8, and 10.

3. how much he expressed feelings verbally (e.g., he may have been experiencing a feeling like sadness, as indicated by his facial expression, but could not express it in words to me);

Table 4.8   Five Measures of Client Affective Experiencing and Expression

Client Measures	2	3	4	5
1. Statements of helplessness	.66	.58	.72	.50
2. Awareness of feelings		.61	.91	.89
3. Expression of feelings			.51	.65
4. Repression				.74
5. "I don't know" statements				

4. how much he repressed his awareness of feelings (e.g., he began to feel sad but then seemed to erase the feeling from consciousness); and

5. how often he said "I don't know" (IDK) when I asked about affect. (I became interested in this assessment when it became apparent that the client frequently made this statement when we were talking about his feelings.)

The matrix in Table 4.8 displays the correlations among all these constructs, based on therapist ratings from 11 sessions.

The two underlined correlations are quite high (> .70), suggesting that the three measures involved (awareness of feelings, repressing feelings, and "I don't know") are assessing a single construct. Thus, these high correlations indicate that awareness of feelings, repressing feelings, and "I don't know" statements could be aggregated into a single score to assess affect. If resources dictated that only one measure be employed, the high correlations indicate that any one of the three measures could be used. My preference, then, would be to employ "I don't know" statements because they require less inference than do the other two ratings.

DATA PATTERNS

All of the analytic methods described in this chapter imply a search for patterns in the data. The patterns in data can also imply certain explanations. Recall (from Chapter 3) Kate's ratings of her client's improvement shown in Figure 4.20.

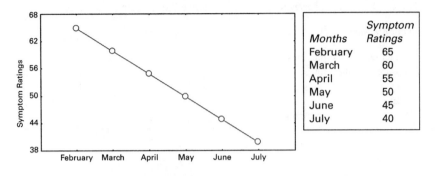

Figure 4.20   Kate's Symptom Ratings of One Client

NOTE: Bland patterns of data may indicate a single cause.

Discussing data patterns in general, Ball (1999) suggested that when a single factor is the cause of the pattern, the resulting data is "one-sided, all form disappears,
and one gets either unstructured, shifting randomness or featureless homogene-
ity—bland in either event" (p. 253). In a sense, our aesthetic reaction to data can
provide hints about its meaning, and the blandness of Kate's ratings suggest that
a single factor (e.g., her desire for her client to improve) could explain these data.
Almost all quantitative data in the social sciences have at least small variations or
natural variability (Larson, 1999). In a clinical context, a lack of variation implies
that the data may not useful for such purposes as measuring change.

Abrupt changes in data suggest that a *threshold* has been crossed and a
new effect has been introduced (Ball, 1999). Luke's jump in anxiety ratings
near termination (Figure 4.13) is an example of a potential threshold. Interest
in *chaos theory* (e.g., Brabender, 2000; Iwakabe, 1999; Masterpasqua &
Perna, 1997) partially stems from its explanations of thresholds in diverse systems and how that might be applicable to understanding nonlinear changes in
human behavior.

Another frequently observed data pattern is a *cycle*. Many types of human
behavior appear to display cyclical patterns. Seasonal Affective Disorder
(SAD; Lee et al., 1998) is a common example: Depression increases during
winter months with a decrease in sunlight, but decreases during summer as the
length of day and amount of sunshine increase. One of the problems compounded by managed care's promotion of brief therapies (Meier & Davis,
2001) is that the length of the treatment period and accompanying data

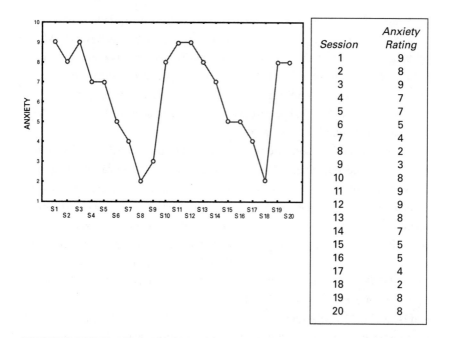

Figure 4.21   Luke's Anxiety Ratings Over 20 Sessions of Psychotherapy

NOTE: "S" stands for session. Cycles of change may be evident when sufficient data have been collected. If Luke's psychotherapy had no effect, the cycle displayed above might appear.

collection period may be too brief to determine if treatment effects are separate from natural cycles (see Hoffman & Meier, 2001). For example, if treatment, in fact, had no effect with Luke, but consisted of 20 sessions instead of 10, the pattern shown in Figure 4.21 might appear.

In situations where multiple outcomes are being assessed, it is quite possible that one or more of them are not affected by treatment. If one or more outcomes are cyclical in nature, sufficient data must be collected for this pattern to become apparent.

COMPUTER SYSTEMS

Although computers are not required for collection and analysis of single case data, they can facilitate these procedures. General purpose word-processing, database management, and spreadsheet programs may be sufficient for many clinicians who may also be familiar with statistical analysis software from graduate school. Even graphing calculators can display time series data. Many of the graphs and basic statistical analyses performed for this book were done with a software program called Statistica (www.statsoft.com); other well-known programs include SPSSx and SAS. The Statistica Web page includes an online statistics text that describes a variety of statistical techniques, including exploratory graphical data analysis.

Clinicians seeking software dedicated to mental health applications will find computer-based outcome, behavioral observation, and clinical charting systems at the Web sites of companies such as Mental Health Outcomes (www.mhoutcomes.com), Psybermetrics (www.psybermetrics.com), Access Measurement Systems (www.ams-outcomes.com), OQ Systems (www.oqsystems.com), PsychSentinel (www.psychsentinel.com), Echo Group (www.echoman.com), CMHC Systems (www.CMHCSystems.com), UNI/CARE Systems (www.UNICARESystems.com), Medical Manager (www.MedicalManager.com), and Centromine (www.Centromine.com), Noldus (www.noldus.com), and Behavioral Health Outcomes Systems (www.bhos.com) (Berman, personal communication, April 10, 2000). Other useful, more general sites related to outcome assessment and data collection include the Joint Commission on Accreditation of Healthcare Organizations site (www.jcaho.org, ORYX section) and the cutting edge efforts of the Ohio Department of Mental Health (www.mh.state.oh.us).

SUMMARY AND CAUTIONS

Because analysis is always concerned with detection of patterns, it is important to recognize that observed patterns may simply be random in nature. The simplest explanation for any pattern of data is *chance* or *randomness* (Abelson, 1995). In other words, so many factors may be influencing what we are measuring that an attempt to attribute causality to one or two factors is misleading. Abelson (1995) noted that most people have a tendency to prefer systematic conclusions to chance as an explanation. This is complicated by the fact that random data patterns can, in small groups of data, resemble data produced by a systematic or causal factor. Even with a fair coin, 5 tosses may produce 5 consecutive tails or heads; a fair coin will not, however, produce 100 consecutive tails or heads.

Abelson (1995) proposed that "systematicity can be claimed when some meaningfully identifiable portions of the data set are markedly different from one another" (p. 22). Thus, efforts to distinguish systematic causes from chance effects will be helped by comparing groups of data affected and unaffected by a systematic cause. For example, data collected during a baseline period can be compared to intervention period data; similarly, data collected from treatment and control groups can be compared to each other at multiple time points. These comparisons of data can allow answers to questions about whether treatment works, as well as how well it works.

Some science-practice approaches suggest that clinicians employ traditional research designs to evaluate their practice. Such methods include the *before-after design* (the A-B design discussed earlier in this chapter), *reversal design, interrupted time series,* and *multiple baselines design* (Streiner, 1998). In an interrupted time series design or A-B design, as described earlier in this chapter, repeated measurements are taken during a baseline period and then an intervention is introduced, with a distinct change of data trends expected if treatment is effective (Streiner, 1998). No formal designs have been advocated in this book, but in philosophy the closest design to what has been advocated here is what Heppner and colleagues (1999) called the *intensive single-subject design*, in which relations among clinical constructs are investigated through systematic and repeated observations.

Clinicians enjoy a wide variety of analytic tools from which to choose methods to examine such questions as the degree of client improvement, the effects of treatment, and the usefulness of case conceptualization and clinical assessment. Although familiarity may largely influence the choice of method, analyses will be enhanced when clinicians can choose from a repertoire of graphical, quantitative, and qualitative methods. In addition, clinicians are better able to interpret analytic results when they are aware of such possibilities as the presence of chance and the meaning of data patterns such as cycles. Nevertheless, errors in clinical judgments and decisions appear inevitable at times, and this topic is the focus of the next chapter.

≠FIVE≠

ALTERNATIVE EXPLANATIONS

———•◦•———

Even if there were not a massive body of research strongly suggesting that clinicians actually have limited capacity to manage complex information and often stumble over a few variables, it should be clear that the obstacles facing the clinician who hopes to integrate all of the data are not merely difficult hurdles, but impossible ones. . . . Perhaps it would not be entirely unfair to say that a large percentage of clinicians do in fact evidence a shared myth about their own judgment capacities. As far as we can tell, there seems to be no plausible way one can legitimately support these beliefs on the basis of scientific evidence.

— Ziskin (1995, p. 261)

The scientist tends to look upon [his or her] assumptions as tentative and problematic and subject to change as . . . observations fail to confirm . . . theoretical expectations.

— Pepinsky and Pepinsky (1954, p. 198)

The core of science is an epistemology or approach to knowledge that accounts for many of the inherent biases in human thought.

— Stoltenberg, Kashubeck-West, Biever, Patterson, and Welch
(2000, p. 632)

As these quotes indicate, mistakes are an unavoidable aspect of clinical work. Although clinicians can make reliable and valid judgments (Garb,

1992), it is also quite easy for them to err during clinical tasks (e.g., Garb, 1998; Nezu & Nezu, 1995; Spengler et al. 1995; Tracey & Rounds, 1999). The important issue here is how we recognize and manage those mistakes.

The first purpose of this chapter is to describe and review problems in the conceptualization, assessment, and analytic domains. Each section includes a description of methods that can help clinicians cope with mistakes and improve future efforts (Faust, 1986; Meichenbaum, 1980). Given that instruction in graduate disciplines such as psychology and medicine has been shown to increase general reasoning skills (Lehman et al., 1988), learning about common clinical errors would seem a useful way to avoid them (Arkes, 1991).

ISSUES IN CASE CONCEPTUALIZATION

Creating a useful case conceptualization is clearly a more difficult task than it first appears. Garb (1998), for example, summarized research that indicated that little consistency exists among clinicians formulating a conceptualization of the same clients. In a study by DeWitt and colleagues (1983), teams of clinicians interviewed the same sets of clients who presented with abnormal grief reactions after the death of a parent. DeWitt and colleagues (1983) found some similarities among the case formulations but concluded that the formulations of treatment teams were not interchangeable. Similarly, Bond and colleagues (1979) found that clients, clinicians, and independent judges did not agree on the content of clients' problems. Other studies have found that agreement among clinicians' conceptualizations has been moderate to poor when (a) clinicians have different theoretical orientations, (b) clinicians have been asked to rate the source of schizophrenic symptoms, and (c) clinicians have been asked to identify client problem areas or nominate a primary target behavior to be changed (Garb, 1998). Also, some clinicians have mistaken the simple presence of certain symptoms (e.g., low self-esteem, depression, suicidal thoughts) as evidence of past sexual abuse (Garb, 1998); improving clinician knowledge of base rates of common and unusual problems may help to avoid errors in this regard (Garb, 1998). Case formulations have also been found to be influenced by client and clinician gender, race, sex roles, age, and religion (Garb, 1998). Garb concluded:

> The reliability and validity of case formulations have been disappointing. For this reason, clinicians should be very careful about making causal judgments.

Because case formulations are frequently made on the basis of clinical experience and clinical intuition, and because reliability and validity have often
been poor for case formulations, clinicians may frequently want to defer
from making judgments about the causes of a client's problems or they may
want to try to use empirical methods to derive causal inferences. (p. 101)

The sheer complexity of human behavior makes creating a case conceptualization a daunting task. Haynes and colleagues (1993) noted that causal relationships in humans are often "nonlinear, bidirectional, conditional, and
dynamic" (p. 282). Many clinical problems appear to be influenced by multiple
causal variables; for example, the research literature on depression indicates
that the variables that control the onset of depression are different from those that
influence the maintenance of depression (Barnett & Gotlib, 1988). In addition,
life stressors may become causal influences on psychological and physical
health only when the stressors pass a critical threshold (Haynes et al., 1993).

When confronting the enormity of the task of case conceptualization, clinicians may take shortcuts. Particularly in the context of what are often difficult
and stressful clinical work environments (Davis & Meier, 2001), clinicians
may have relatively little time or energy for thinking clearly or deeply about
clients. If clinicians lack adequate resources for conceptualization tasks, however, a number of problems may result, the most important of which is
described next.

Hypothesis Confirmation Bias

The *hypothesis confirmation bias* (HCB) refers to the tendency to pay
attention to information that confirms our initial expectations and to ignore
other, disconfirming information. Clinicians, like laypersons, may inappropri-
ately crystallize on early impressions of other people (Darley & Fazio, 1980;
Hoshmand, 1994; Jones, Rock, Shaver, Goethals, & Ward, 1968; Snyder &
Swann, 1978; Tracey & Rounds, 1999). HCB appears limited to our own
ideas: Haverkamp (1993) found that clinicians were more likely to employ
confirmatory biases when they self-generate a hypothesis about a client than
when the hypothesis is provided via a client's statement of the problem.

If you have attended case conferences, you will likely have had the experience of a clinician deciding on a diagnosis and course of treatment within
5 to 10 minutes of a client description. If clinicians' initial impressions are cor-
rect, subsequent inquiry and intervention will be useful. But when hypotheses

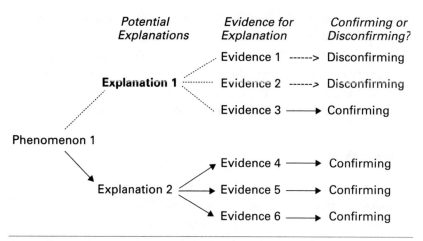

Figure 5.1   How HCB Influences Judgment

are misleading or incorrect, interviewers are likely to ignore important information that is contrary to their initial impression. As Murphy and Davidshofer (1988) observed, "there is a pervasive tendency to overestimate the accuracy of one's judgments, and clinicians do not seem to be immune from this tendency" (p. 374).

Figure 5.1 indicates that for any phenomenon, two or more possible explanations exist, and that for any particular explanation, several pieces of evidence exist that may confirm or disconfirm that explanation. If the HCB occurs, the observer will choose a single explanation and attend only to the confirming evidence. Suppose that for a phenomenon two explanations are apparent, as in Figure 5.1. For the first explanation, three pieces of evidence are collected to test that explanation, and two appear to disconfirm the explanation. Three pieces of evidence are collected for the second explanation and all these support the explanation. Given that more evidence supports Explanation 2, a choice between the two is straightforward. However, a person who has decided before the evidence is collected that Explanation 1 is true will be more likely to ignore or discount the two pieces of disconfirming evidence and emphasize the one piece of supporting evidence found for that explanation. In fact, a person convinced that the first explanation is true may pay no attention to any evidence around the second explanation.

The major problem created by HCB is that it short-circuits the feedback loop of conceptualization, assessment, and analysis of intervention effects.

That is, our theoretical blinders can keep us from observing and processing relevant clinical information that could help us to help modify and improve the therapeutic process (Hoshmand, 1994). HCB is a potential explanation for Bickman and colleagues' (2000) finding that most clinicians do not have alternative treatment plans for failing clients: These clinicians appear unaware that they can conceive of other ways of thinking about failing clients.

Coping With HCB

The most common recommendation is to develop alternative explanations, ideas different from those initially employed in the case conceptualization (Garb, 1998; Spengler et al., 1995; Tracey & Rounds, 1999). In terms of clinical process, what are other elements that could account for change? Obvious sources of alternative constructs are different psychotherapy schools, intake and progress notes, and the research literature relevant to the client's presenting problems. For example, a young adult male who presented with a social phobia was making slow but steady progress through a systematic desensitization program. About halfway through the program, however, he mentioned in passing several conversations with his mother regarding the progress he was making. Although the therapist did not consider family influences at that point, it would have been a wise move. Without warning, the client dropped out of therapy on his mother's recommendation.

Also consider Tsui-Ling, a 28-year-old married international student from Taiwan complaining of low energy and being unable to complete her dissertation (Grieger & Ponterotto, 1995; Meier, 1999). Tsui-Ling had recently suffered a miscarriage late in the second trimester and subsequently displayed such depressive symptoms as lack of energy, difficulty concentrating, fatigue, and sleep disturbance. Clinical work with Tsui-Ling proceeded from a cognitive-behavioral approach to depression, which included educating her about depression and the possible psychological effects of significant life events. In mid-December, at the end of her academic semester, Tsui-Ling terminated. In February, however, Tsui-Ling reappeared, again complaining of the same type and severity of depression as when she began therapy 6 months before. Tsui-Ling reported that she had had past episodes of severe depression, during previous Februaries, that had then lasted for months. Upon further probing, Tsui-Ling recalls that her father had died unexpectedly 3 years ago, in February. After the session, a review of notes from Tsui-Ling's September

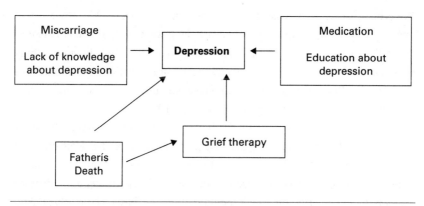

Figure 5.2   Alternative Explanations for Tsui-Ling's Depression and
Interventions

NOTE: This is one possible process-outcome model for Tsui-Ling. Her miscarriage and lack of
knowledge about depression form one group of potential causes for her depressive symptoms.
Tsui-Ling's father's death is an alternative explanation for her depression.

intake indicates that she had described the circumstances surrounding her
father's death as well as her strong reaction to it.

Two explanations for a clinician's missing the importance of Tsui-Ling's
father's death include HCB and overshadowing. The HCB is the probable
explanation if the clinician had crystallized early on the miscarriage as the
only cause of Tsui-Ling's depression and ignored or forgotten other clues,
such as past episodes of depression around the time of her father's death.
Another judgment problem, *overshadowing*, occurs when a client presents
with multiple problems, but one problem appears so significant to the clinician
that others are missed. A typical finding in overshadowing research is that a
person with mental retardation is less likely to be diagnosed with a coexisting
mental disorder than is a person without mental retardation (see, e.g.,
Spengler & Strohmer, 1994). Thus, for the clinician, Tsui-Ling's recent miscarriage may have overshadowed her father's more distant death.

To avoid HCB or overshadowing with Tsui-Ling, the original case conceptualization should be modified to include both her miscarriage and her father's
death as potential influences on her depression. As shown in Figure 5.2, several
interventions could target both of these events to alleviate her depression.

The HCB may also account for why some clinicians historically have
maintained stereotypes on the basis of gender, race, or culture (e.g.,

Broverman, Broverman, Clarkson, Rosenkrantz, & Vogel, 1970; Swenson & Ragucci, 1984). Some clinicians, for example, have been found to equate cultural differences with deficiencies (Rollock & Terrell, 1996). Pathology may be assigned where none is warranted by the client's situation in the context of the client's cultural norms; an overemphasis on culture, however, may result in a failure to identify pathology (Ridley et al., 1998).

In addition to constructing alternative explanations, other suggestions for combating HCB include making specific predictions, delaying decisions, and keeping raters blind to hypotheses. By making a prediction about future events, we establish an explicit test for deciding whether to keep, modify, or abandon the explanation on which the prediction was based (Hill, 1991). And a major part of the problem with HCB is a rush to judgment: By delaying a diagnosis or case conceptualization, we may be able to accumulate more information to inform the task (Dumont & Lecomte, 1987; Ridley et al., 1998; Sandifer, Hordern, & Green, 1970). Also, allowing ideas to incubate can result in the recall of additional important information, as well as in the surprise connection of previously unrelated concepts (O'Neill, 1993). Finally, if assessment of conceptualization constructs can be conducted by persons blind to the clinical hypotheses, this may also minimize HCB effects (Hill, 1991).

Check Predictive Validity

If a client model is valid in a traditional sense, predictions can be made on the basis of the model that can be checked against future events (O'Neill, 1993). Predictions made on the basis of client models should be as specific and concrete as possible. Predictions may not be immediately observable—the predictor and future event may be separated by a chain of events—but should become so at some reasonable future point. As shown in Figure 5.3, a clinician may predict that doing family therapy with a 13-year-old boy with failing grades will lead to an increase in those grades.

However, such a prediction is likely to be invalid for most adolescents because it does not account for factors other than family influences that could account for grades. On the other hand, family therapy, as shown in Figure 5.4, might benefit communication among family members, members' social skills, and the parents' relationship.

Family therapy might have a relatively indirect effect on the boy's grades by providing more parental supervision of homework and a more stable

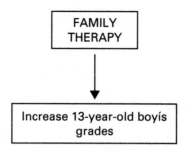

Figure 5.3   Will Family Therapy Increase a 13-Year-Old's School Grades?

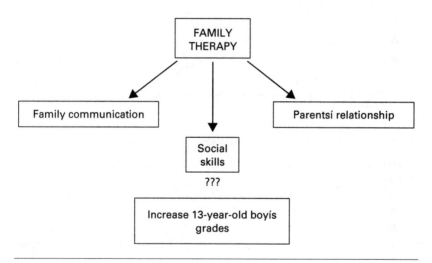

Figure 5.4   What Can Family Therapy Influence?

NOTE: Family therapy might influence intermediate outcomes that eventually lead to an increase in the boy's grades.

home environment. For many students, a stable family may be a necessary but insufficient condition for improving academic performance.

More important influences on the boy's grades might be his intellectual ability, study skills, and motivation to succeed in school, factors unlikely to be directly impacted by family therapy. Thus, if future events predicted by the

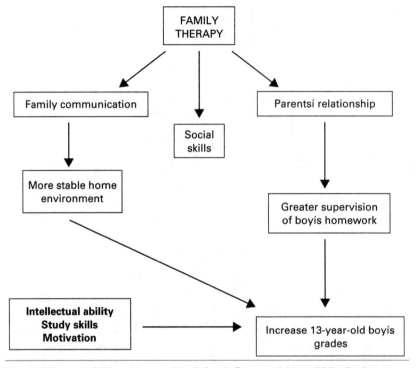

Figure 5.5   Additional Factors Needed to Influence 13-Year-Old's Grades

NOTE: Although family therapy may lay the foundation, more immediate factors are likely to influence school grades.

model do not occur, then a reconsideration and modification of the original model may be warranted.

Consider Client Strengths

One of the problems introduced by the advent of third-party payment for psychotherapy, and particularly reinforced by managed care, is the emphasis on symptomatology and the medical model in clinical work. In fact, managed care companies employ "medical necessity" as the basic criterion for deciding whether treatment will be provided and reimbursed (Davis & Meier, 2001). *Medical necessity* refers to some threshold where services are deemed necessary for the diagnosed condition (Davis & Meier, 2001).

Even with clients who possess severe difficulties, however, client strengths and resources should be considered part of the case conceptualization. For example, Linehan (1993) indicated that the first two assumptions about implementing Dialectical Behavior Therapy (DBT) with borderline clients are that (a) they are doing the best they can and (b) they want to improve. Holding these assumptions while creating case conceptualizations and the treatment plan can open the clinician to new possibilities. For example, emphasizing skills training as a part of the therapeutic intervention can engage client resources and motivation and enhance the possibility of obtaining desired outcomes. When communicated to clients, these assumptions can remove some of the debilitating self-blame clients experience as well as return to clients a sense of control (Meier & Davis, 2001). Emphasizing client strengths is also one of the major techniques employed in crisis intervention, again as a method of enhancing clients' sense of control (Greene, Lee, Trask, & Rheinscheld, 2000).

Be Aware of Clinician Differences in Conceptualization Skills

Cognitive characteristics appear to be related to conceptualization problems. Spengler and Strohmer (1994) found that psychologists with lower cognitive complexity were more likely to form biased clinical judgments. *Cognitive complexity* refers to the use of a more versatile, multidimensional construct system; complex clinicians tend to ask more questions of clients and consider a wider range of hypotheses before reaching a diagnosis. Similarly, Martin and colleagues (1989) found that experienced clinicians possess "extensive abstract, general knowledge of counseling that they use to conceptualize specific instances of counseling efficiently and parsimoniously" (p. 395). Novice clinicians tend to "engage in more extensive, unique conceptual work for each separate client" (Martin et al., 1989, p. 395). Counseling students' conceptual level also has been related to the quality and clarity of their clinical hypotheses (Holloway & Wolleat, 1980). Some evidence suggests that adding structure to clinical work can improve the performance of less complex clinicians (see Berg & Stone, 1980; Holloway, 1995; Stoltenberg, McNeill, & Delworth, 1998).

ISSUES IN CLINICAL ASSESSMENT

As with conceptualization, clinical assessment tasks can be difficult to perform well. For example, research has found little agreement among pairs of clinicians asked to judge the appropriate level of care needed for children and adolescents (Bickman, Karver, & Schut, 1997). In one study, clinicians' descriptions of an actor being interviewed about work experiences varied from "realistic" and "enthusiastic," when they were told the man was being interviewed for a job, to "defensive," "hostile," and "depressed," when they were told he was a patient (Langer & Abelson, 1974). Garb (1998) reviewed studies that found that clinicians could be susceptible to *primacy effects* (i.e., making judgments quickly, with minimal data) and *anchoring and adjustment effects* (using different starting points yields different estimates).

Evaluating Reliability

Recall that *reliability* refers to the consistency of a test or assessment procedure. A measurement or assessment that produces consistent data is said to be reliable. For example, if you completed the same intelligence or personality test two times, a week apart, and basically obtained the same scores both times, this would constitute evidence of test-retest reliability.

Because evaluations of reliability partially depend on the properties of the construct being measured, evaluating the reliability of data produced by measures of clinical constructs can be problematic. Recall the distinction made in Chapter 3 between *traits* (enduring psychological characteristics) and *states* (characteristics that change). If you are measuring cognitive abilities, they probably will remain stable, at least over relatively short periods of time. Many of the clinical constructs you will assess, however, are expected to show variability. When you implement an intervention, for example, process and outcome measures are likely to evidence change. If no variation is present with measures of constructs expected to change, one possibility is that the measures are insensitive to change. In this case, assessments that produce data with little or no variability should be modified or dropped unless there exists a reasonable expectation of change at some future time.

So how do you evaluate the reliability of a measure expected to show change, that is, to evidence inconsistent scores over time? With a measure containing multiple items, you can calculate a measure of internal consistency, coefficient alpha. *Coefficient alpha* can be considered the average correlation of all items in a test intended to measure one construct. Support for internal consistency is evident if the items correlate highly with each other. For example, a single client might complete the OQ-45 10 times over the course of therapy.

After entering all item responses for the 10 completions, alpha can be then computed with statistical analysis software such as SSPSx; values above .70 are considered adequate evidence of reliability for scores produced with that measure (Meier & Davis, 1990).

Several other procedures may be more applicable for evaluating the consistency of clinical assessments of individual clients. First, if you are recording data from a session audiotape, listen to the tape a second time and repeat the assessment. Provide a sufficient time interval so that you do not remember the original assessment data, and then repeat the assessment procedure. For example, suppose you audiotape sessions with an individual client who tends to use the phrase "I don't know" when he begins to become aware of emotionally threatening material. You may count the number of "I don't know"s after listening to the tape once and then again a few days later. If the two counts differ, a factor or factors other than the construct you intended to measure are influencing the data.

Another option is to ask another person to perform the same assessment. If your client is self-monitoring, for example, instruct her or him to request a friend or family member to assess the same construct independently. In alcohol treatment settings, a spouse could record the alcohol consumption of the client. If the clinician provides data, a supervisor or colleague could corroborate the assessment by watching sessions through a one-way mirror or by observing an audiotape or videotape.

Effects of the Assessment Method

As noted in Chapter 3, the data produced by any particular assessment depend not only on the content of the item or task but also on the method used (see Campbell & Fiske, 1959). For example, if a client reports on level of anxiety during a session, and the therapist rates the client on level of anxiety during the same session, differences in the data will be present simply because of the different sources. Interestingly, client reports of the benefits of psychotherapy are usually lower than ratings by therapists and expert judges (Lambert, 1994). This presents the problem of knowing which method provides more valid information. Because often no definitive answer to this question exists, psychotherapy outcome researchers tend to measure change from multiple perspectives, including self-reports and therapist ratings of behavioral, affective, and cognitive constructs (Lambert, 1994).

Cummings, Hallberg, Slemon, and Martin (1992) found a more complex interaction regarding the effect of method on therapists' and clients' recall of events that occurred during therapy sessions. For sessions that clients had rated as effective, Cummings and colleagues (1992) found that clients (not therapists) had more accurate recall of events. For all therapeutic events, however, therapists had more accurate recall. Analyses also indicated that client and therapist were more likely to recall the same important event from the sessions that had been rated as more effective.

The issue of method is particularly relevant when discussing the validity of process and outcome assessments. If both sets of assessments employ the same method, then the relation between the constructs may be artificially inflated. If you have a self-report method of measuring process and a self-report method of measuring outcome, for example, the resulting correlation will be higher than if either process or outcome were measured via a different method. If resources allow, the best solution is to measure a construct using two or more methods. For example, you might measure a student's aggressive behaviors through self-report, parent rating, and teacher rating. Aggregating the scores for these assessments across methods may provide a better measure of aggression than data from any single assessment alone.

The Effect of a Single Measure

Although the use of two methods may improve the reliability and validity of scores on an assessment, the sum of two different measures that employ the same method may also do so. Because data produced by any single test or assessment will contain random error, two assessments of the same construct, when aggregated, will reduce the effect of that error (Epstein, 1979).

Suppose you are assessing depression at the end of each session with two self-report measures, the Beck Depression Inventory-2 and the MMPI-2 Depression Scale. Averaging those scores is likely to present a better measure of depression than will scores from either alone. Both scales are likely to contain some, and possibly different, flaws; hypothetically, the BDI-2 may be more difficult for your client to understand, whereas the MMPI-2 takes longer and may lead to more fatigue for and less effort by the client. Aggregating the two is likely to balance the different errors and provide a more reliable and valid estimate of depression.

Recall the discussion in Chapter 3 of Kate, the graduate student who provided the symptom ratings for one client. Suppose this client was experiencing

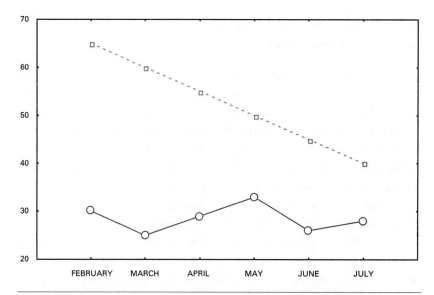

Figure 5.6   Symptoms and Minutes Late Per Session for Kate's Client

NOTE: A better sense of outcome for Kate's client could be obtained by obtaining information from a second source (e.g., the client or a significant other) or from a second measure provided by the same source (shown above). This graph suggests that although Kate's ratings of symptoms (dashed line) decreased over time, the number of minutes her client was late for therapy sessions (solid line, summed per month) stayed about the same.

work-related difficulties, one aspect of which was that she was frequently late to work. As a proxy measure, Kate could record how many minutes late this client was for each therapy session and then total that number for each month for comparison of trends with symptom ratings (see Figure 5.6).

Thus, consider obtaining the second measure via a different method than the first. While Kate's ratings of symptoms appear relatively open to influence by her desire to appear credible, a simple recording of when the client arrived for the session requires less inference on Kate's part. Figure 5.6 suggests that while Kate's ratings of symptoms show improvement over time, the number of minutes late the client appears for therapy sessions does not evidence change.

As with this example of Kate's client, it may be particularly important to include more than one measure of outcome. Interventions have multiple outcomes: To the extent that interventions are efficacious, they are likely to produce changes in different directions and in multiple domains.

Do Not Mistake a Single Behavior or
Unit of Measurement for a Construct

This problem is an interaction between assessment and conceptualization where an assessor fails to realize that a single operation or type of operation does not totally reflect one construct. For example, Carlson and Grotevant (1987) noted that although theoretical conceptualizations about family inter-action describe *patterns* of family behavior, family interaction researchers tended to focus solely on *rates of behavior*. Marital relationship quality, for example, could be assessed by counting the frequency of compliments between partners as well as by graphing sequences of the initiation of conver-sations, washing dishes, or taking care of the children.

Cone (1988) distinguished between *molecular behaviors* and *molar behaviors*: The latter represent a group of behaviors that reflect a construct, such as anxiety, whereas the former are very specific behaviors (e.g., hair-pulling) that individually do not represent the total problem. Cone recom-mended examining the correlation between measures of the molar and molecular behaviors to see which of the molecular behaviors relate most closely to the whole problem. Although one or more highly correlated molec-ular behaviors can serve as proxies for the molar behavior, it is important to remember that a molecular behavior is not the client's central problem. The client's problem in this example is anxiety and its manifestations, not simply hair-pulling.

Systematic Errors

The history of psychological measurement and assessment contains ample documentation of systematic errors that affect assessment data (Meier, 1994). Such errors include:

1. *Response styles*, acting in a particular direction regardless of the assessment content (e.g., saying "yes" to all questions regardless of content);

2. *Response sets*, behavior designed to generate a particular impression (e.g., socially desirable responding);

3. *Random responding*, completing items or tasks without intention (e.g., checking self-report items at random);

4. *Dissimulation*, faking good or bad; and,

5. *Malingering*, exaggerating psychological conditions.

Social desirability is a type of response set, that is, a tendency to respond with answers that the respondent believes are most socially acceptable or make the respondent look good (Edwards, 1953; Lanyon & Goodstein, 1982; Nunnally, 1967). Although social desirability has been researched primarily with personality tests, the phenomenon has also been noted with other measurement methods, including the clinical interview. Barlow (1977) described a patient who came to treatment with problems of anxiety and depression that the patient indicated were associated with social situations. Over a 1-year period, the patient made progress in a treatment that emphasized his learning social skills, but he still complained of anxiety and depression. Finally, the patient blurted out that the basic cause of his discomfort was the strong feelings of homosexual attraction he experienced in some social situations. When the client was asked why he did not report this previously, "he simply said that he had wanted to report these attractions all year but was unable to bring himself to do so" (p. 287). Although homosexuality may not be the taboo subject it once was, issues surrounding such sensitive topics as sexuality and substance abuse remain subject to social desirability bias. Hser, Anglin, and Chou (1992), for instance, found that self-reports of male addicts showed greater inconsistency between two interviews for more socially undesirable behaviors, such as narcotics use, than for socially desirable behaviors, such as employment.

Reactivity

Reactivity refers to whether the degree of transparency of a measurement alters the resulting data. For example, suppose we wish to determine how many hours students studied for a particular test. The manner in which this information is obtained may affect the resulting data. Students could self-monitor their study hours; however, self-monitoring has been shown to increase desirable behaviors (Nelson, 1977a, 1977b). If students' reports were linked to some type of reward (e.g., extra credit), we could expect reports of even more studying, in some cases independent of how much studying actually took place. Finally, without the students' knowledge, we could instruct roommates or family members to record how often they observed the students

Table 5.1   Factors Influencing Reactivity

More Reactivity ◄————————►	Less Reactivity
Behavioral rating tasks	Global rating tasks
Interpretation of behavior	Recording simple presence or absence of behavior
Retrospective reports	Real-time reports
Untrained observers	Trained observers
Assessment on a single occasion	Multiple assessment
Assessment involves personal significance	Assessment involves little personal significance for the observer
No incentives for accurate information	Incentives for accurate information present

SOURCES: Paul (1986) and Meier (1994).

studying, although they would probably observe only some of the studying and consequently provide underestimates.

More transparent methods may be altered in ways favorable to the person being assessed. As shown in Table 5.1, reactivity has been linked to the personal significance of the assessment task, the presumed intent of the task (particularly if the task is evaluative), and the incentives for providing accurate information (Meier, 1994; Paul, 1986).

Clinical researchers (Garb, 1998; Kerig, 2001; Meier, 1994; Paul, 1986) have recommended several steps to reduce or prevent the effects of reactivity. Just as adding structure to clinical interviews appears to enhance their reliability (Meier, 1994), the following steps can be viewed as adding structure to any type of measurement method:

1. *Increase reliance on informants who are part of the client's environment.* Staff, spouses, parents, and fellow students all form potential sources of collaboration.

2. *Obtain data from multiple sources, which differ in reactivity.* Would the report of the parents of a particular child, for example, be more or less likely to distort the child's number of study hours than reports by the child's friends or siblings?

3. *Allow subjects to adapt to observations before formal data collection.* In psychophysiological recording, subjects typically are allowed a few minutes to get accustomed to the sensors and monitoring equipment.

Similarly, clients and therapists require some time before they begin to ignore audiotape or videotape equipment in a therapy room.

4. *Create engaging tasks that are both face valid and reasonable for the observer to perform.* If possible, select assessment tasks that appear directly related to the client's problem. Providing a clear rationale for assessment can also help in this regard.

5. *Train and monitor assessors.* Clearly specify the behaviors to be observed and the conditions under which assessment will take place. Provide assessors with practice and in vivo rating practice. Track assessors' performance and provide feedback regularly.

6. *Minimize recording delays.* Record behavior as soon as possible. As explained below, a delay between when a behavior occurs and when it is recorded can translate into error.

Another approach to consider is *unobtrusive measurement,* in which individuals are unaware that measurement is occurring (Kazdin, 1980; Meier & Wick, 1991; Webb, Campbell, Schwartz, Sechrest, & Grove, 1981). By definition, unobtrusive measures handle the problem of reactivity. Examples of unobtrusive measurement include simple observation in naturalistic settings, observation in contrived situations (e.g., simulations, laboratories), examination of archival records, and obtaining physical traces. However, unobtrusive measures can be costly and present potential ethical problems, particularly in clinical settings (Meier, 1994).

Drift, Decay, and Recording Delays

In assessments using ratings, *drift* refers to systematic changes in definition or interpretation of a construct; *decay* occurs with similar, but random changes. Both drift and decay negatively affect the reliability of assessments. Decay may be evidenced by slight variations over time that show no particular trends. Drift should evidence a more orderly or distinct change in data. Particularly when examining small time intervals, assessors must be careful not to overinterpret such small changes, particularly as evidence of treatment effectiveness.

Figure 5.7 displays client data that evidences slight changes over time. If these were Luke's anxiety ratings, the simplest explanation for this pattern of

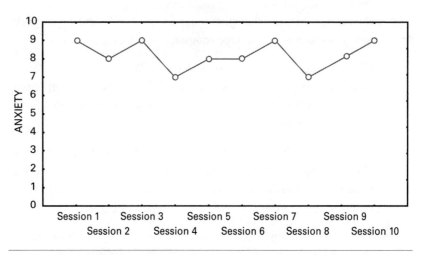

Figure 5.7   Data Explained By Decay

NOTE: Decay may be the simplest explanation for small, apparently random changes in clinical data.

variation would be chance or decay. That is, relatively little systematic variation appears to be evident.

Prevention is the best method for dealing with drift and decay. Four steps (Hartman, 1984; Meier, 1994) can be useful:

1. *Provide a clear rationale to the assessors.* Specify what it is that assessors should be paying attention to. For example, a seemingly straightforward task of counting how many questions Carl Rogers asked in a videotape of a counseling session was complicated by the fact that many of Rogers's paraphrases sounded like questions (e.g., "So you felt sad?") (Meier, 1994). It might have been better to record only those questions meant to obtain new information from the client.

2. *Train assessors.* Assessors should receive some training and instruction on the assessment task. Provide practice rating sessions as well as discussions of the rating process with other raters and instructors. Such efforts may clarify ambiguous parts of the assessment task and result in the rewriting and clarification of the assessment instructions.

3. *Monitor procedures.* Find some method of checking the reliability of the assessors. In training, you can provide assessors with a task simulating the

actual assessment situation. With an actual intervention that has been taped, check reliability by replaying the tape to rerate the assessment. Assessors who know that their data are being evaluated are more likely to produce reliable and valid data.

4. *Get converging evidence.* Consider alternate methods for obtaining assessment data. For example, you might have two raters assess the same behavior and then compare the data for consistency (e.g., ask the client and spouse to monitor alcohol consumption).

Problems with decay may be linked to a delay between when an event occurs and its observation or recording. As the amount of time increases between when a person observes an event and when he or she records it, the reliability of the observation decreases (Paul, 1986). The longer anyone in the assessment process takes to record data, the more likely she or he is to forget or distort data. If you tape a session or record the event immediately after it happens in session, no problem with recording delay exists. If you do not or cannot tape the session or record the event during the session, produce your assessment as soon as possible after the session. If clients or others produce the assessment, instruct them to record the information without delay. In general, question your memory when recalling clinical events (Garb, 1998).

Halo Effects

Halo refers to a generalized schema or belief system that restricts the range of assessment data (Meier, 1994; Saal, Downey, & Lahey, 1980). In plainer language, halo errors occur when an assessor's stereotype blinds the assessor to discrepant information. For example, a teacher may decide that a particular person is a "good student" and ignore evidence that says otherwise. In college, I enrolled in a class that included a series of weekly essay quizzes graded by the instructor. I studied a great deal for the first several weeks and received high grades. One week, however, I studied very little and completed what I thought was a poor quiz. Expecting a low grade, I was surprised the following week to receive a quiz with about the same grade I had received in the previous weeks. In hindsight, my guess is that the instructor had decided that I was a "good student" and expected that I would do good work (regardless of the quality of the work I actually did). These halo errors can be found in employment and clinical situations as well.

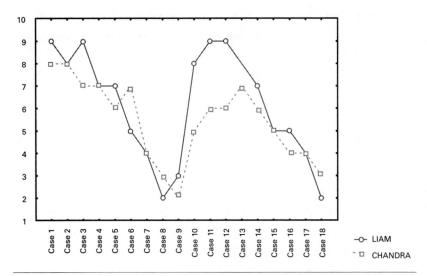

Figure 5.8   Evidence of Halo Effects With Two Consecutive Clients

NOTE: Because global ratings may be influenced by halo effects, clinician ratings with consecutive clients may evidence substantial covariation.

Two solutions for halo errors involve awareness of the problem and blind assessment. Staying aware of the possibility of potential (and perhaps unusual) variability in the phenomenon under investigation may help assessors avoid halo errors. In some circumstances, it may also be helpful if the assessor is blind to the identity or other important characteristics of the observed person (e.g., gender, age, race) so as to avoid stereotyping.

Because halo errors may be particularly prevalent in global ratings, one method for evaluating the degree of halo is to compare the global ratings of two or more clients. Halo may be enhanced if the clinician interacts with the clients on the same day or during consecutive sessions. Figure 5.8 displays a clinician's global rating for two clients, Liam and Chandra, seen in consecutive sessions once a week.

The two client ratings in Figure 5.8 evidence considerable covariation (the correlation equals .83), raising doubts about their validity. While two clients who began therapy at the same time may show a similar course of treatment, it is more likely that the covarying patterns shown in Figure 5.8 were significantly influenced by the therapist's mood or perceptions of the concurrent client. In addition, multiple ratings of one client on two or more global dimensions (e.g., functioning, symptomatology) may also evidence covariation problems.

Special Problems With Behavioral Assessment

With behavioral observations of frequency, an assessor can be overwhelmed with the resulting quantity of data. Without an audio or video recording of a session, for example, attempts to count classes of verbal behavior (e.g., statements such as "I don't know") may be inaccurate unless these events occur infrequently. *Continuous recording* of behavior (i.e., recording all behaviors or every instance of a particular behavior) should occur only when the event of interest is of low frequency or sufficient resources are available for this demanding task. If the behaviors are moderate to high frequency or sufficient resources are unavailable, another alternative is to sample behaviors according to a predetermined schedule (Hartman, 1984; Paul, 1986).

In contrast to *event sampling* strategies (where all low frequency, critical behaviors are recorded), *time sampling* strategies require the assessor to record behavior according to a schedule. *Random sampling* refers to observing behavior at random time points. For example, if you wanted to count the number of times a client said a certain phrase (e.g., "I feel anxious") during a 45-minute counseling session, you might divide the session up into nine 5-minute intervals and then randomly choose three or four intervals in which to count. This would decrease the difficulty of maintaining a count of the behavior during the entire session and, by observing randomly, increase the likelihood that the samples of behavior would adequately reflect the construct of interest. *Interval recording* refers to observing behavior at specified periods of time. A clinician might believe that the beginning and end of a session are the most anxious periods for a particular client. If anxiety was related, for example, to the number of disruptions of normal speech patterns (Mahl, 1987), the clinician might observe more disruptions in the first and last 5 minutes of a session than the middle 5-minute interval. Both random and interval sampling allow an assessor to minimize expenditure of resources and obtain useful data. Nevertheless, individual segments of a session may not reflect the tremendous variability of client and therapist activity that occurs within a single session (Hill, 1991).

Be Aware of Clinician Differences in Assessment Skills

Some evidence suggests that therapists differ in their assessment skills (e.g., in their ability to provide valid ratings of treatment progress; Battle et al., 1966). Observational skills tend to increase with age and are often better developed in women and persons with better social skills, intelligence, motivation, and attention to detail (Meier, 1994). As with conceptualization, training assessors can improve performance (Hill, 1991). As noted earlier in this chapter, a number of authors have suggested steps for improving clinical ratings. Paul (1986) discussed the training of raters for his assessment system and suggested that they (a) be provided with and learn an observation manual (including definitions of behaviors to be measured and scoring procedures), (b) conduct analogue observations, (c) practice in real-life situations, and (d) receive occasional retraining, feedback, and debriefing.

ISSUES IN ANALYTIC JUDGMENTS

The focus here is on judgment problems that occur when clinicians attempt to interpret clinical data. Three problems are discussed below: Casual (not causal) analyses, small data samples, and clinical versus actuarial prediction.

Casual Analyses

After clinical assessment data are collected, clinicians may simply eyeball or browse the data instead of conducting more structured analyses. As Kazdin (1999) noted, however, "years of research have shown that humans, whether or not they are clinicians, cannot adequately assess processes or changes and relations among variables through casual and informal observations" (p. ix).

O'Brien (1995) found empirical support for the dominance of casual analyses in a study of eight clinical psychology graduate students. They were presented with hypothetical self-monitoring data related to a client's process and outcome factors (displayed in Table 5.2 below). As shown in Figure 5.9, the outcomes were number of headaches, headache severity, and headache duration; the process elements were the number of stressors, number of arguments, and hours of sleep. Students were instructed to "evaluate the data 'as they normally would' in a clinical setting" (O'Brien, 1995, p. 352). Seven of

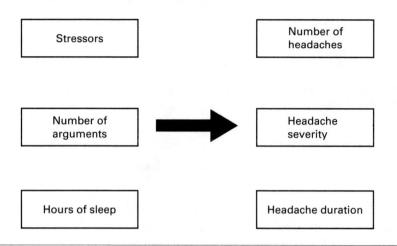

Figure 5.9 Process and Outcome Elements in a Client with Headaches

Table 5.2 Hypothetical Self-Monitoring Data Reported Over 14 Days By a Client Suffering From Headaches

	Process Measures			Outcome Measures		
Day	Number of Stressors	Number of Arguments	Hours of Sleep	Number of Headaches	Headache Severity	Headache Duration
1	3	7	8	4	9	1
2	6	1	6	3	5	3
3	5	3	9	6	5	2
4	8	1	5	7	1	4
5	4	2	7	1	6	4
6	7	2	6	5	4	3
7	2	2	8	2	4	1
8	7	5	4	5	7	6
9	2	2	8	3	6	2
10	7	3	5	5	9	3
11	5	3	8	4	6	1
12	3	1	7	5	6	2
13	7	3	7	7	5	1
14	5	3	6	6	8	2

SOURCE: "Inaccuracies in the Estimation of Functional Relationships Using Self-Monitoring Data," by W. H. O'Brien, 1995, *Journal of Behavior Therapy and Experimental Psychiatry, 26,* pp. 351-357. Copyright © 1994 by Elsevier Science. Adapted with permission.

Table 5.3   Correlations Computed for Hypothetical Self-Monitoring Data

	Outcome Measures		
Process Measures	*Number of Headaches*	*Headache Severity*	*Headache Duration*
Number of Stressors	.63	.25	.51
Number of Arguments	.08	.65	.06
Hours of Sleep	.30	.00	.77

SOURCE: O'Brien (1995).

NOTE: These correlations suggest that different process elements are related to different outcome constructs.

the eight students reported that they eyeballed the data, while one computed correlation coefficients among the process and outcome factors. O'Brien found that the students' intuitive judgments consistently underestimated the size of the functional relationships in the data.

What could the students have done instead of eyeballing? Computing the actual correlation coefficients (Table 5.3) is simple if you have access to basic statistical software. As shown in Table 5.3, the correlation between headaches and stressors equals .63, while the correlation between headaches and arguments is .08.

Simpler yet would be to draw one or more time series plots (by hand or with a computer program) of the process and outcome variables. O'Brien also studied the relations between headache frequency and number of stressors and arguments, which are illustrated in Figure 5.10.

Small Data Samples

Special attention should be paid to the problem of the small samples of data present in many clinical situations. With small samples of outcome assessments, for example, it is difficult to separate chance effects from treatment effects. Although we may feel more comfortable with small amounts of data (Faust, 1986), in general the more data collected, the better the chances of drawing valid conclusions. In addition, research on human judgment shows that people have difficulty assessing covariation, making use of base rates, and recognizing regression toward the mean (Faust, 1986). Faust (1986) concluded that "people's limited capacities to use more than small amounts of information effectively . . . place major barriers on their attempts at integration" (p. 424). For the statistically sophisticated, several newer statistical methods may be of use in clinical analyses with

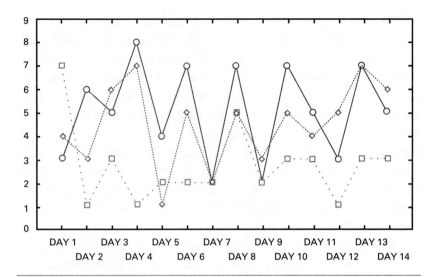

Figure 5.10   Multiple Time Series for Number of Stressors and Number of Arguments With Headache Frequency

NOTE: The line plots indicate that the number of headaches (circles with dashed line) appears to be more closely related to the number of stressors (circles with solid line) than to the number of arguments (squares with dashed line).

small samples (Hoyle, 1999). In general, analyses with small data sets (less than 10 observations per construct) should be interpreted with caution.

Clinical Versus Actuarial Prediction

A basic problem with clinical judgment is clinicians' tendency to downplay the importance of information other than their judgment. Two general conclusions can be drawn from the well-known literature on clinical versus statistical prediction. First, statistical prediction usually equals or outperforms clinical judgment (e.g., Meehl, 1954; Dawes, Faust, & Meehl, 1989; Wedding & Faust, 1989). Second, many clinicians ignore the first conclusion and are overconfident in their judgment (Arkes, 1991; Einhorn & Hogarth, 1978). This may result from the lack of useful feedback clinicians receive about their clinical performances as well as the judgment habits and cognitive limitations found in most people (Faust, 1986; Garb, 1998).

The extensive literature on clinical versus actuarial prediction (Dawes et al., 1989; Meier, 1994; Murphy & Davidshofer, 1994) continues to provide evidence that although clinicians can be useful generators of causal hypotheses and collectors of data related to those hypotheses, they rarely combine data in an optimal manner for predictive purposes. Mossman (1994), for example, found that statistical prediction slightly bested clinical judgment in the long-term prediction of violence. Faust (1986) suggested that clinical judgment problems may partially account for the superiority of tests over clinical judgment. In studies where clinician behavior is examined, clinicians often appear unreliable: When given the same information on two or more occasions, clinicians reach different conclusions (Meier, 1994). Garb (1998) concluded: "When methodologically sound research has been conducted, clinicians should weight the empirical results more heavily than they weigh their own clinical experiences" (p. 234).

In many clinical situations, however, data about a predictor-criterion relation may not exist. For example, there exists little data to predict how successful therapy will be with any particular client. And even when such data exist, the predictive power of the data may be fairly low. For example, clinicians would be unwise to make predictions about particular clients' likelihood to commit suicide or homicide *solely* on the basis of test scores, even if those scores were the result of tests created and validated to predict suicidal or homicidal behavior. As Allport (1937) noted, what is also needed is an idiographic understanding of the factors likely to influence that person's behaviors in different situations.

SUMMARY

Subjective judgments are unavoidable in clinical work, and they can be influenced by numerous biases (Haynes et al., 1993). The basic purpose of this book is to provide a structure that augments clinical judgment and minimizes errors. Planned, systematic examination of relevant client behaviors, based on a case conceptualization, is likely to improve most clinicians' judgment performances. In addition, increased awareness of common problems in clinical judgment, along with methods for coping with these limitations, should also aid clinical decision making. The major coping method discussed in this chapter involves holding ideas tentatively and being open to the possibility of changing ideas as disconfirming data appear. From the start of work with all clients, then, we should strive to be conscious of alternative explanations.

SIX

POSSIBLE FUTURES

————•◦•————

A s evidenced in the first five chapters of this book, important benefits can occur when clinical science and practice are interwoven. Even in the helping professions, however, history repeats itself. Without a substantial force changing the clinical professions, current practice will become future practice. Recent changes in clinical practice have often been less focused on quality than on amount or type of therapy. For example, the major effect of managed care on psychotherapy has been to shorten the number of sessions delivered, constrain costs, and move therapists toward cognitive-behavioral orientations and techniques (Davis & Meier, 2001). No current evidence indicates that managed care has improved clinical outcomes (Davis & Meier, 2001).

The first section of this chapter describes a number of paths that might be taken to make progress on the science-practice agenda. Clinical research would also benefit if researchers paid more attention to the problems clinicians face when attempting to employ research methods and the results of research in their daily work. Thus, the second half of the chapter discusses a set of basic clinical research problems that remain to be addressed.

HOW CHANGE MIGHT OCCUR

A better integration of science and practice might occur if action were taken to upgrade professional standards in this area; alter student selection criteria; teach differently; create specialists in conceptualization, measurement, and analysis; increase the use of computer technology in practice; encourage a group of science-practice innovators to promote greater integration; and provide monetary incentives for better integration. Each suggestion is discussed below.

Upgrade Professional Standards

The simplest approach to greater integration may be to upgrade expectations about how science can be a useful component of clinical practice. For example, professional standards might specify how conceptualization and assessment should be integral to intervention. Standards could describe various "evaluation models that integrate continuous collection, analysis, and reporting of data seamlessly into practice routines" (Nugent et al., 2001, p. 383). Thus, standards might explain how to use knowledge about current research and practice guidelines (such as those provided by empirically validated procedures) but would also include descriptions of how to employ scientific procedures (see Cape & Parry, 2000). This book describes one such set of procedures; other models of science-practice integration have been provided, for example, by Barlow, Hayes, and Nelson (1984); Heppner and colleagues (1992); Nugent and colleagues (2001); and Stricker and Trierweiler (1995).

Upgrading professional standards would prompt subsequent discussions about changing educational standards and curriculum. Future planning about clinical training should include the extent to which we expect clinicians to be able to perform conceptualization and assessment tasks competently. Although clinicians perform work that is often emotionally intense, clinical educators and supervisors can have low expectations of students with regard to the more abstract conceptualization and assessment tasks.

Alter Student Selection Criteria

A basic problem with the integration of science and practice centers on the vocational interests of the people entering the helping professions. According to Holland's (1997) RIASEC (Realistic, Investigative, Artistic, Social, Enterprising, Conventional) theory, counselors and therapists have strong Social interests: Their primary motivation for work is to interact and develop relationships with others. In contrast, scientific professions attract individuals with Investigative interests who like to study and explore research-related subjects. Holland (1997) indicated that adults can be described in terms of two or three primary vocational interests, such as SAI (Social, Artistic, Investigative, found in librarians and speech pathologists) or SIA (Social, Investigative, Artistic, found in clinical and counseling psychologists). Such interest clusters enhance the chances of successful careers in matching vocations.

Clinical educators might focus greater attention on attracting and admitting students whose second or third dominant vocational interest is Investigative in nature. The likely result of a systematic attempt to admit such students would be clinical training programs that graduate scholarly clinicians. Although they would not necessarily be producers of research publications, these professionals would understand and value research to the extent that they employ systematic methods and current knowledge in their practice.

Teach Differently

As noted in Chapter 1, learning occurs in specific situations and is not easily decontextualized (Gentile, 1990); transfer of learning is enhanced when learners identify and employ underlying principles in new contexts. A student who can complete a master's thesis or dissertation, for example, may still lack both the motivation and knowledge to apply scientific methods in practice. Rather than assume that students will transfer what they learn in research and analysis courses to practice settings, conceptualization, assessment, and analysis should be explicitly taught in clinical and practicum courses (Meier, 1999). Such an approach explicitly acknowledges the Social vocational interests of students who choose the helping professions and adds scientific methods to the clinical mix.

Although teaching graduate students a science-practice approach can improve their self-efficacy for conceptualization and assessment tasks (Meier, 1999), considerable individual variability is likely to be evident in students' skills. My experience as an instructor is that many students struggle with basic applications, such as creating a client model, and need frequent feedback from the instructor and other students. Fearing critical feedback, some students also resist close supervision of their work (see Tracey, Ellickson, & Sherry, 1989). In contrast, skilled students select more abstract constructs for their client models and employ these models to guide their clinical work.

Create Specialists in Conceptualization, Measurement, and Analysis

Because it may simply be impractical to ask clinicians to gather the amount and quality of information necessary to assess process and outcome elements and conduct subsequent analyses, another approach involves the creation of educational programs that provide training in one or more of the areas of conceptualization, measurement, and analysis. Such training could be the entire focus of a minor specialty in doctoral training or a postdoctoral specialization. The resulting professionals would not be full-time direct service providers, but rather, would be specialists who produce or evaluate clinically relevant information and provide intervention-related feedback to clinicians.

Mash and others (Mash, 1991; Mash & Barkley, 1986; Mash & Hunsley, 1993; Mash & Foster, 2001; Groth-Marnat, 2000) have previously proposed the creation of *assessment centers* that would function similarly to medical laboratories. Measurement and assessment tasks, along with data analysis and reporting of results, would be shared among clinicians as well as technicians and professionals working in such centers. Information related to treatment progress from various methods and sources would be fed back to clinicians. Increased use of the Internet and continued investment in computer hardware and software in most practice settings make such approaches feasible; for example, some behavioral assessment tasks and situations may now be computer administered (e.g., Jongsma, Peterson, & McInnis, 2001; Meier & Wick, 1991). In addition to specialists in medicine, other precedents exist for such specialists in the helping professions. Behavioral assessors, for example, are an integral part of the social learning system employed in Paul's inpatient treatment system (Paul, 1986). Also, many of the practitioners and researchers who publish in such journals as *Assessment, Measurement and Evaluation in Counseling and Development* and *Psychological Assessment* possess the required expertise for such a specialty.

Increase the Use of Computer Technology in Practice

In many practice settings, computers already facilitate storage of clinically-relevant quantitative and qualitative data. The role of technology in augmenting scientific approaches in clinical practice, however, may become much more significant in the future. Kozak (1996), for example, envisioned computer programs that could keep track of all the possible problems that a patient may present with or all of the relevant information necessary for managing a given problem. The computer can rapidly and accurately exhaust combinatorial reasoning for any given problem presentation, coupling the unique features of the patient with what is known about these features from the scientific literature. (p. 1335)

A computer system that could record and transcribe the spoken interactions between clients and clinicians would be a significant enhancement to qualitative methods that researchers and practitioners could employ to examine clinical process and outcome (see Mergenthaler & Kachele, 1996). The development and widespread dissemination of such systems, morever, might result in a significant decrease in the use of self-report measures of outcome. With self-reports, clients must translate their personal experiences into numbers, which are then analyzed and eventually translated back into qualitative statements about their progress or lack thereof. Although likely to incorporate quantitative elements, a system for summarizing and interpreting therapeutic conversations might take the place of many self-report procedures.

Encourage a Group of Science-Practice
Innovators to Promote Greater Integration

Another approach would be to assemble a group of helping professionals, educators, and scientists who engage in, teach, or research practice-science approaches. To the extent that such a group would regularly exchange ideas and conduct demonstrations and studies that investigate the potential benefits of such an integration, it could be a powerful force for innovation. Although some professional groups are interested in science-practice integration (e.g., the Academy of Psychological Clinical Science at http//w3.arizona.edu/~psych/apcs/apcs.html or the Society for a Science of Clinical Psychology at http://pantheon.yale.edu/~tat22/), many professionals have relatively few venues (e.g., dedicated journals, listservs, conferences) for meeting and collaborating on creative approaches. Building on the work of previous conferences (Belar & Perry, 1992; Peterson et al., 1991), practice-science conferences that result in the creation of ongoing working groups might be one way to jumpstart such enterprises. These groups could focus on the creation of procedures and products such as books, tests, Web sites, and software that could be of practical use to clinicians. As Clement (1999) noted about the collection and analysis of outcome information, "the usefulness of the information needs to outweigh the additional work" (p. 10).

Provide Monetary Incentives for Better Integration

If financial incentives were attached to the use of scientific methods in practice, integration efforts would quickly accelerate. For example, the frequency of traditional psychological testing has declined under managed care (Eisman et al., 2000); if managed care companies require outcome assessments, clinicians or clients typically complete them without additional reimbursement. If clinicians possessed reasonably valid methods to provide data relevant to client change and the additional resources necessary to perform these tasks, significant savings might be obtained through the provided feedback (e.g., Lambert et al., 2001). Clinicians can now easily manipulate tools such as the GAF to make it appear that clients need additional sessions—and it is difficult to criticize them for doing so, given that many managed care companies often appear to deny services primarily for their own profit. If managed care companies became as focused on effectiveness as they are on constraining costs (Clement, 1999; Davis & Meier, 2001), their interest in promoting scientific approaches would increase. Various pieces of healthcare legislation that have been considered in the U.S. Congress (which include the right to sue insurers) might provide such motivation.

Other options exist with respect to resources. Grant money to stimulate research examining the potential benefits of greater science-practice integration might provide a more focused approach to this effort. Also, by raising the cost of using less optimal strategies, the higher stakes may result in less superficial treatment of conceptualization, assessment, and analysis tasks (Arkes, 1991). One way to raise the stakes might be to use systems that highlight treatment success and failure: Some states, for example, make public information on hospital and surgeons' success rates for medical procedures. Should success rates for agencies and licensed clinicians also be made available?

OBSTACLES TO CHANGE

Three of the most significant obstacles to furthering a practice-science combination are a lack of resources, traditional clinical culture, and the need for research about science-practice approaches.

Perhaps the largest impediment to implementing further integration is the lack of resources to support it. No funding sources are currently in place for financing measurement specialists or paying clinicians to collect and analyze outcome data. At a time when managed care has reduced the medical budget devoted to mental health—to about 4% of medical claims, down from 10% in 1990 (Kessler, 1998)—any factor that increases cost in the short term will likely be opposed or ignored even if it were to lead to long-term increases in efficiency. Although an unexpected development (such as a proposal for a national health insurance program) could change this picture quickly, no solution to the problem of procuring the additional resources required for science-practice integration currently appears in sight.

In addition, in many clinical settings few traditions or norms exist to support scientific practices. Having completed their graduate training, many clinicians (like faculty) seldom receive systematic feedback about the effectiveness of their work. For example, only about 20% of psychologists measure outcomes (Clement, 1999), and evaluation is typically not a component of social work practice (Rosen, 1992). Mark and colleagues (1991) noted clinicians' initial resistance to the implementation of a record-keeping system; clinicians made such statements as "it makes us feel uncomfortable that we are being watched" (p. 1165). There also remains an undercurrent of belief among some students and clinicians that important outcomes in psychotherapy cannot be measured in *any* meaningful or useful way (see Gottman & Leiblum, 1974). As discussed below, research on the benefits and costs of science-practice integration might begin to change beliefs about the usefulness of scientific approaches in counseling and psychotherapy.

Finally, relatively little research has been done to support the hypothesis that integrating science into practice improves clinical process or outcomes. Such research would be complex and difficult, but empirical investigation could further refine the integration in the helping professions. I discuss in the next section a set of questions that would benefit from further study.

RESEARCH INTO SCIENCE-PRACTICE INTEGRATION

Five major domains related to the integration of clinical science and practice would benefit from further investigation: general effects, conceptualization, assessment, data collection and analysis, and education and training. Potential questions within these areas are described below.

General Effects of Integrating Clinical Science and Practice

Broadly speaking, what effects do science-practice integrations produce?

1. Does the additional structure of scientific methods produce measurable effects on clinical process or outcome?

2. Are clinicians who employ scientific methods more cost effective? For example, do clinicians who collect outcome assessment regularly do a better job of terminating appropriately with clients?

3. On the other hand, are scientifically oriented clinicians seen by clients as less empathic or trustworthy? Are they seen as more expert?

4. Are clinicians who integrate science more effective with failing clients? Students in my clinical courses have observed that in many instances of clients' failure to make progress, the major influences were outside the therapeutic realm. This means that in some cases clinicians can do little to avoid failure.

5. Does use of idiographic methods produce better or different outcomes than using nomothetic approaches? Does an idiographic approach, for example, provide a better method for preventing treatment failure? Can idiographic and nomothetic approaches be employed to complement each other? Paralleling the argument made here, Hayes (1995) suggested that clients failing empirically supported treatments (ESTs) provided by master's level clinicians might be referred to doctoral level therapists who could institute a more idiographic approach.

6. How do resource issues affect the use of integrative methods? For example, in settings with fewer resources, are nomothetic self-reports more likely to be employed?

7. Do clinicians who integrate science into practice have different levels of job satisfaction or professional development?

8. When used with clients of color, do idiographic methods, compared to nomothetic approaches, produce better conceptualizations, more reliable and valid data, or better outcomes?

Integrating Conceptualization Into the Clinical Process

The work of Dansereau and colleagues (e.g., Chmielewski & Dansereau, 1998) provides evidence supporting the benefits of incorporating visual maps into the clinical process. Related questions include:

1. What effects do different methods of case conceptualization produce on clinical process or outcome? How much does the "truth" of the conceptualization matter in regard to outcomes? Can different conceptualizations of a single client result in comparable outcomes?

2. Should conceptualizations be shared with clients? If so, when and how? Do visual displays help in this process?

3. What perspectives on causality are most helpful? In some sense the helping professions now seem pulled between a traditional positivist view, where reality is seen as truth waiting to be discovered, and a constructivist perspective, where reality is viewed as socially created. Maloney and Ward (1976) proposed the idea of *conceptual validity* where constructs and hypotheses are evaluated in terms of their usefulness for understanding a client's functioning. Also, O'Neill (1993) suggested that clinical inference is best demonstrated by showing that one explanation answers a question better than others do and that the explanation predicts subsequent events.

Integrating Assessment Into the Clinical Process

Researchers such as Bloom and colleagues (1992) and Lambert and colleagues (2001) have conducted studies that suggest that providing regular feedback to clients about outcomes can improve those outcomes. Related questions include:

1. Do clinicians who employ outcome assessments in their practice uniformly evidence better outcomes? Do these outcomes differ, for example, for clients who initially are making progress or failing?

2. Does providing feedback about outcomes improve outcomes more than other methods, such as clinical supervision or reviewing audiotapes?

3. What idiographic methods are best for improving clinicians' understanding of clients, ability to predict future behavior, and client outcomes?

4. Do idiographic methods benefit from standardization, as happens when interviews become more structured (Meier, 1994)?

Methods for Data Collection and Analysis

Mark and colleagues (1991; see Lyons & Payne, 1974) cited studies indicating that medical practitioners who keep better records also provide better care. But many questions remain about data collection:

1. How often should assessment data be collected and fed back to clinicians? To clients, supervisors, or utilization reviewers?

2. Do different purposes of feedback, such as improving services or managing costs, have different effects on clinical process and outcome?

3. What are the best methods for recording, storing, displaying, and analyzing clinical data? Mark and colleagues (1991) substituted a structured record-keeping system for an unstructured one in a clinic and found improved record keeping.

4. What is the best method for recording and recalling progress notes? What kind of information can be extracted from such notes?

5. What information might provide useful feedback about the quality of the data collection system? For example, should agencies or individual clinicians receive report cards about the amount and quality of information they collect? Agencies and practitioners who now conduct outcome assessments seldom have procedures for checking the quality of the collected data (Meier & Letsch, 2000). Also, what factors influence rates of missing data (Meier & Letsch, 2000)? And, does adding "administrative mechanisms for the quality control of [a] measurement system" (Kiresuk, Choate, Cardillo, & Larsen, 1994, p. 106) improve clinical process or client outcomes?

6. How might redundancy in data collection systems (e.g., multiple intake procedures, different amount measures by funding agency) be reduced?

The Best Approaches to Education and Training

Little research has been conducted to investigate the best methods of teaching students or clinicians about integrating science into practice. Questions include:

1. What combination of personality characteristics and training environment will produce the best scientist-practitioners (e.g., Kahn & Scott, 1997)? For example, does the presence of Investigative vocational interests predict which students will be most likely to employ scientific methods and knowledge effectively in their practice?

2. Which science-related products (e.g., procedures, tests, videos, books, software) are most useful to clinicians? What factors might foster acceptance of scientific innovations in practice?

The science-practice perspectives pursued in these questions may also illuminate other puzzling findings in the clinical literature. For example, Weisz, Weiss, Han, Granger, and Morton (1995) found that psychotherapy studies conducted in laboratories and clinics produce stronger effects than studies conducted in field settings such as community agencies. Such results led to a distinction between *efficacy studies* (conducted in controlled, laboratory settings) and *effectiveness studies* (conducted in field settings). Laboratory studies, however, typically involve more homogenous client populations (i.e., persons who are recruited and treated for depression or specific types of anxiety or phobia) whose outcomes are detectable with nomothetic measures. Detecting treatment effects among the heterogeneous client populations found in agencies and clinics, however, may require idiographic measures. Applying nomothetic measures with a diverse client population experiencing a wide range of treatment effects will result in effects that are diffuse and small when aggregated across the items of nomothetic measures (much like random error in the aggregation of items on a scale). In addition, debate continues about the relative contribution of specific versus common factors in psychotherapy (Wampold, 2001). Again, the net result of employing nomothetic measures to detect idiographic changes in a heterogeneous client sample is that the great variety of idiographic changes exhibited by individual clients are diffused throughout the nomothetic items. Thus, specific factors will be difficult to detect, leaving common factors as a default explanation. An alternative explanation, however, is that counseling and psychotherapy produce idiographic effects that are neither common across clients nor specific to particular diagnoses or psychotherapy schools.

CONCLUSION

Pursuing a science-practice agenda in clinical, research, and training arenas opens up an exciting range of challenges and opportunities. Current efforts to integrate science and practice tend to focus on *empirically validated treatments* (EVTs) or *empirically supported treatments* (ESTs) and their accompanying manuals. These methods employ the results of randomized clinical trials, comparing treatment and control groups to specify the most efficacious treatments for particular problems or diagnoses. Working with a client whose problem can be categorized into a diagnosis with an accompanying EST, the EST conceptualization and intervention is likely to represent the best starting point from an actuarial perspective (see Jacobson et al., 1989; Schulte, Kunzel, Pepping, & Schulte-Bahrenberg, 1992; Wilson, 1996).

Although arguably the best-known method of science-practice integration now available, empirically supported approaches also have limitations (Eifert et al., 1997; Nathan, 1998; Strupp & Anderson, 1997). First, besting a control group represents a significant, but relatively common accomplishment: Most psychotherapies show superior outcomes when formally compared to controls. Second, the amount of change found in EST outcome studies can be relatively small. Westen and Morrison (2001) conducted a meta-analysis of 34 efficacy studies of treatments of depression, generalized anxiety disorder, and panic disorder. Among their results was the finding that only 37% of clients who began clinical treatment for depression showed improvement. Westen and Morrison maintained that (a) ESTs were effective for only about half of clients, who were themselves carefully selected so as to possess only the diagnosis of interest, and (b) many of those who made gains in treatment lost them over time. In addition, ESTs tend to ignore important aspects of clinical culture and situations. ESTs apply to general diagnostic categories, use specific therapeutic techniques, and emphasize adherence to a treatment manual; in contrast, clinicians in most practice settings tend to focus on an individual client and the therapeutic relationship while valuing treatment flexibility (Addis, Hatgis, Soysa, Zaslavsky, & Bourne, 1999; Jacobson et al., 1989).

Further merging of the cultures of scientific research and clinical practice is necessary. Developers of ESTs might shape their products toward a more traditional clinical framework; likewise, clinicians would benefit from increased attention to evidence-based practices, greater openness toward evaluation, and acknowledgement of the reality of clinical errors. Illustrations of such mergers are present in this book and in similar works, including Beutler and Harwood (2000), Persons (1989), and Wilson (1996). Improving clinical judgment and client outcomes through better use of scientific methods and research remains the goal of those who endeavor in this field.

REFERENCES

Abelson, R. P. (1995). *Statistics as principled argument*. Hillsdale, NJ: Lawrence Erlbaum.

Acuff, C., Bennett, B., Bricklin, P., Canter, M., Knapp, S., Moldawsky, S., & Phelps, R. (1999). Considerations for ethical practice in managed care. *Professional Psychology: Research and Practice, 30*, 563-575.

Addis, M. E., Hatgis, C., Soysa, C. K., Zaslavsky, I., & Bourne, L. S. (1999). The dialectics of manual-based treatment. *The Behavior Therapist, 7*, 130-132.

Aftanas, M. S. (1994). On revitalizing the measurement curriculum. *American Psychologist, 49*, 889-890.

Allport, G. W. (1937). *Personality*. New York: Henry Holt.

Allport, G. W. (1942). *The use of personal documents in psychological science* (Bull. No. 49). New York: Social Science Research Council.

American Psychiatric Association. (1994). *Diagnostic and statistical manual of mental disorders* (4th ed.). Washington, DC: Author.

American Psychological Association. (1993). Record keeping guidelines. *American Psychologist, 48*, 984-986.

Argyris, C. (1976). Theories of action that inhibit individual learning. *American Psychologist, 31*, 638-654.

Arkes, H. R. (1991). Costs and benefits of judgment errors: Implications for debiasing. *Psychological Bulletin, 110*, 486-498.

Babor, T. F., Brown, J., & Del Boca, F. K. (1990). Validity of self-reports in applied research on addictive behaviors: Fact or fiction? *Behavioral Assessment, 12*, 5-31.

Babor, T. F., Stephens, R. S., & Marlatt, G. A. (1987). Verbal report methods in clinical research on alcoholism: Response bias and its minimization. *Journal of Studies on Alcohol, 48*, 410-424.

Ball, P. (1999). *The self-made tapestry*. Oxford, UK: Oxford University Press.

Bandura, A. (1977). Self-efficacy: Toward a unifying theory of behavioral change. *Psychological Review, 84*, 191-215.

Bandura, A. (1986). *Social foundations of thought and action: A social cognitive theory*. Englewood Cliffs, NJ: Prentice Hall.

Bandura, A. (1997). *Self-efficacy: The exercise of control*. New York: Freeman.

Barlow, D. H. (1977). Behavioral assessment in clinical settings: Developing issues. In J. D. Cone & R. P. Hawkins (Eds.), *Behavioral assessment* (pp. 283-307). New York: Brunner/Mazel.

Barlow, D. H., Hayes, S., & Nelson, R. (1984). *The scientist practitioner.* New York: Pergamon.

Barnett, P. A., & Gotlib, I. H. (1988). Psychosocial functioning and depression: Distinguishing among antecedents, concomitants, and consequences. *Psychological Bulletin, 104*, 97-126.

Battle, C. C., Imber, S. D., Hoehn-Saric, R., Stone, A. R., Nash, E. R., & Frank, J. D. (1966). Target complaints as criteria of improvement. *American Journal of Psychotherapy, 20*, 184-192.

Beail, N. (Ed.). (1985). *Repertory grid technique and personal constructs.* London: Croom Helm.

Beck, A. P., & Lewis, C. M. (2000). *The process of group psychotherapy: Systems for analyzing change.* Washington, DC: American Psychological Association.

Beck, A. T. (1976). *Cognitive therapies and the emotional disorders.* New York: International Universities Press.

Beck, A. T., Emery, G., & Greenberg, R. L. (1985). *Anxiety disorders and phobias: A cognitive perspective.* New York: Basic Books.

Beck, A. T., Rush, A. J., Shaw, B. F., & Emery, G. (1979). *Cognitive therapy of depression.* New York: Guilford.

Beck, J. (1995). *Cognitive therapy: Basics and beyond.* New York: Guilford.

Bednar, R. L., & Kaul, T. J. (1994). Experiential group research: Can the canon fire? In A. E. Bergin & S. L. Garfield (Eds.), *Handbook of psychotherapy and behavior change* (4th ed., pp. 631-663). New York: John Wiley.

Belar, C., & Perry, N. (Eds.). (1992). National Conference on Scientist-Practitioner Education and Training for the Professional Practice of Psychology. *American Psychologist, 47*, 71-75.

Berg, K. S., & Stone, G. L. (1980). Effects of conceptual level and supervision structure on counselor skill development. *Journal of Counseling Psychology, 27*, 500-509.

Bergin, A. E., & Garfield, S. L. (Eds.). (1994). *Handbook of psychotherapy & behavior change.* New York: John Wiley.

Berman, P. (1997). *Case conceptualization and treatment planning.* Thousand Oaks, CA: Sage.

Beutler, L. E. (2000). Empirically based decision making in clinical practice. *Prevention & Treatment, 3*, Article 27. Retrieved December 1, 2000, from http://journals.apa.org/prevention/volume3/toc-sep01-00.html

Beutler, L. E., & Hamblin, D. L. (1986). Individualized outcome measures of internal change: Methodological considerations. *Journal of Consulting and Clinical Psychology, 54*, 48-53.

Beutler, L. E., & Harwood, T. M. (2000). *Prescriptive psychotherapy: A practical guide to systematic treatment selection.* Oxford, UK: Oxford University Press.

Bickman, L., Karver, M. S., & Schut, L. J. (1997). Clinician reliability and accuracy in judging appropriate level of care. *Journal of Consulting and Clinical Psychology, 65*, 515-520.

Bickman, L., Rosof-Williams, J., Salzer, M., Summerfelt, W. T., Noser, K., Wilson, S. J., & Karver, M. (2000). What information do clinicians value for monitoring adolescent client progress and outcomes? *Professional Psychology: Research and Practice, 31*, 70-74.

Biggs, D. A. (1988). The case presentation approach to clinical supervision. *Counselor Education and Supervision, 28*, 240-248.

Binder, J. L., & Strupp, H. H. (1997). Supervision of psychodynamic psychotherapies. In C. E. Watkins, Jr. (Ed.), *Handbook of psychotherapy supervision* (pp. 44-62). New York: John Wiley.

Blau, T. H. (1988). *Psychotherapy tradecraft: The technique and style of doing therapy.* New York: Brunner/Mazel.

Blocher, D. H. (1987). *The professional counselor.* New York: Macmillan.

Bloom, L. A., Hursh, D., Wienke, W. D., & Wolf, R. K. (1992). The effects of computer assisted data collection on students' behavior. *Behavioral Assessment, 14*, 173-190.

Bloom, M., & Fischer, J. (1982). *Evaluating practice: Guidelines for the accountable professional.* Englewood Cliffs, NJ: Prentice Hall.

Boeker, H., Hell, D., Budischewski, K., Eppel, A., Hartling, F., Rinnert, H., von Schmeling, F., Will, H., Schoeneich, F., & Northoff, G. (2000). Personality and object relations in patients with affective disorders: Idiographic research by means of the repertory grid technique. *Journal of Affective Disorders, 60*, 52-59.

Bond, G., Bloch, S., & Yalom, I. (1979). The evaluation of a "target problem" approach to outcome measurement. *Psychotherapy: Theory, Research, and Practice, 1*, 48-54.

Borders, L. D., Bloss, K. K., Cashwell, C. S., & Rainey, L. M. (1994). Helping students apply the scientist-practitioner model: A teaching approach. *Counselor Education and Supervision, 34*, 172-179.

Brabender, V. (2000). Chaos, group psychotherapy, and the future of uncertainty and uniqueness. *Group, 24*, 23-32.

Brody, G. H., & Forehand, R. (1986). Maternal perceptions of child maladjustment as a function of the combined influence of child behavior and maternal depression. *Journal of Consulting and Clinical Psychology, 54*, 237-240.

Brookfield, S. (1990). *The skillful teacher.* San Francisco: Jossey-Bass.

Broverman, L., Broverman, D., Clarkson, E., Rosenkrantz, P., & Vogel, S. (1970). Sex-role stereotypes and clinical judgments of mental health. *Journal of Consulting and Clinical Psychology, 34*, 1-7.

Brown, T., & Barlow, D. (1995). Long-term outcome in cognitive-behavior treatment of panic disorder: Clinical predictors and alternative strategies for assessment. *Journal of Consulting and Clinical Psychology, 63*, 754-765.

Burn, B., & Payment, M. (2000). *Assessments A to Z.* San Francisco: Jossey-Bass.

Burns, D. D., & Nolen-Hoeksema, S. (1991). Coping styles, homework assignments, and the effectiveness of cognitive-behavioral therapy. *Journal of Consulting and Clinical Psychology, 59*, 305-311.

Butcher, J. N. (1990). *Assessing patients in psychotherapy: Use of the MMPI-2 for treatment planning.* New York: Oxford University Press.

Cacioppo, J. T., & Tassinary, L. G. (1990). Inferring psychological significance from physiological signals. *American Psychologist, 45*, 16-28.

Campbell, D. T., & Fiske, D. W. (1959). Convergent and discriminant validity by the multitrait-multimethod matrix. *Psychological Bulletin, 56*, 81-105.

Cape, J., & Parry, G. (2000). Clinical practice guidelines development in evidence-based psychotherapy. In N. Rowland & S. Goss (Ed.), *Evidence-based counselling and psychological therapies: Research and applications* (pp. 171-190). London: Routledge.

Carlson, C., & Grotevant, H. D. (1987). A comparative review of family rating scales: Guidelines for clinicians and researchers. *Journal of Family Psychology, 1*, 23-47.

Chmielewski, T. C., & Dansereau, D. F. (1998). Enhancing the recall of text: Knowledge mapping training promotes implicit transfer. *Journal of Educational Psychology, 90*, 407-413.

Christensen, A., Margolin, G., & Sullaway, M. (1992). Interparental agreement on child behavior problems. *Psychological Assessment, 4*, 419-425.

Chwalisz, K. (2001). A common factors revolution: Let's not "cut off our discipline's nose to spite its face." *Journal of Counseling Psychology, 48*, 262-267.

Clark, D. A. (1999). Case conceptualization and treatment failure: A commentary. *Journal of Cognitive Psychotherapy: An International Quarterly, 13*, 331-337.

Clement, P. W. (1994). Quantitative evaluation of 26 years of private practice. *Professional Psychology: Research and Practice, 25*, 173-176.

Clement, P. W. (1999). *Outcomes and incomes.* New York: Guilford.

Cone, J. D. (1988). Psychometric considerations and the multiple models of behavioral assessment. In A. S. Bellack & M. Hersen (Eds.), *Behavioral assessment: A practical handbook* (3rd ed., pp. 42-66). Elmsford, NY: Pergamon.

Cone, J. D. (1989). Is there utility for treatment utility? *American Psychologist, 44*, 1241-1242.

Cone, J. D. (2001). *Evaluating outcomes: Empirical tools for effective practice.* Washington, DC: American Psychological Association.

Cook, T. D., & Campbell, D. T. (1979). *Quasi-experimentation.* Chicago: Rand McNally.

Corcoran, K., & Gingerich, W. J. (1994). Practice evaluation in the context of managed care: Case-recording methods for quality assurance reviews. *Research on Social Work Practice, 4*, 326-337.

Corey, G. (1996). *Theory and practice of counseling and psychotherapy* (5th ed.). Pacific Grove, CA: Brooks/Cole.

Corsini, R., & Wedding, D. (1995). *Current psychotherapies* (5th ed.). Itasca, IL: F. E. Peacock.

Creswell, J. W. (1994). *Research design: Qualitative and quantitative approaches.* Thousand Oaks, CA: Sage.

Creswell, J. W. (2002). *Educational research.* Upper Saddle River, NJ: Merrill-Prentice Hall.

Cronbach, L. J. (1984). *Essentials of psychological testing* (4th ed.). New York: Harper & Row.

Cronbach, L. J., & Gleser, G. C. (1965). *Psychological tests and personnel decisions* (2nd ed.). Urbana, IL: University of Illinois Press.

Cross, K. P., & Angelo, T. A. (1988). *Classroom assessment techniques.* Ann Arbor, MI: National Center for Research to Improve Postsecondary Teaching and Learning.

Cummings, A., Hallberg, E., Martin, J., Slemon, A., & Heibert, B. (1990). Implications of counselor conceptualizations for counselor education. *Counselor Education & Supervision, 30,* 120-134.

Cummings, A., Hallberg, E., Slemon, A., & Martin, J. (1992). Participants' memories for therapeutic events and ratings of session effectiveness. *Journal of Cognitive Psychotherapy: An International Quarterly, 6,* 113-124.

Czuchry, M., & Dansereau, D. F. (1998). The generation and recall of personally relevant information. *Journal of Experimental Education, 66,* 293-315.

Darley, J., & Fazio, R. (1980). Expectancy confirmation processes arising in the social interaction sequence. *American Psychologist, 35,* 867-881.

Davis, S., & Meier, S. (2001). *The elements of managed care.* Pacific Grove, CA: Brooks/Cole.

Dawes, R. M., Faust, D., & Meehl, P. E. (1989). Clinical versus actuarial judgment. *Science, 243,* 1668-1674.

DeWitt, K. N., Kaltreider, N. B., Weiss, D. S., & Horowitz, M. J. (1983). Judging change in psychotherapy: Reliability of clinical formulations. *Archives of General Psychiatry, 40,* 1121-1128.

DiClemente, C. C., & Prochaska, J. O. (1985). Processes and stages of change: Coping and competence in smoking behavior change. In S. Shiffman & T. A. Wills (Eds.), *Coping and substance abuse.* New York: Academic Press.

Dobson, K. (1989). A meta-analysis of the efficacy of cognitive therapy for depression. *Journal of Consulting and Clinical Psychology, 57,* 414-419.

Dumont, F., & Lecomte, C. (1987). Inferential processes in clinical work: Inquiry into logical errors that affect diagnostic judgments. *Professional Psychology: Research and Practice, 18,* 433-438.

Duncan, O. D. (1985). Path analysis: Sociological examples. In H. M. Blalock, Jr. (Ed.), *Causal models in the social sciences* (2nd ed., pp. 55-79). Hawthorne, NY: Aldine.

Edwards, A. (1953). The relationship between the judged desirability of a trait and the probability that the trait will be endorsed. *Journal of Consulting Psychology, 24,* 90-93.

Eells, T. D. (1997). (Ed.). *Handbook of psychotherapy case formulation.* New York: Guilford.

Egan, G. (1998). *The skilled helper: A problem-management approach to helping* (6th ed.). Pacific Grove, CA: Brooks/Cole.

Eifert, G. H., Schulte, D., Zvolensky, M. J., Lejuez, C. W., & Lau, A. W. (1997). Manualized behavior therapy: Merits and challenges. *Behavior Therapy, 28*, 499-509.

Einhorn, H. J., & Hogarth, R. M. (1978). Confidence in judgment: Persistence of the illusion of validity. *Psychological Review, 85*, 395-416.

Eisman, E. J., Dies, R. R., Finn, S. E., Eyde, L. D., Kay, G. G., Kubiszyn, T. W., Meyer, G., & Moreland, K. L. (2000). Problems and limitations in using psychological assessment in the contemporary health care delivery system. *Professional Psychology: Research & Practice, 31*, 131-140.

Eldridge, W. D. (1993). *Conceptualizing the evaluation of clinical counseling.* Lanham, MD: University Press of America.

Elliott, R. (1998). Editor's introduction: A guide to the empirically supported treatments controversy. *Psychotherapy Research, 8*, 115-125.

Epstein, S. (1979). The stability of behavior: I. On predicting most of the people much of the time. *Journal of Personality and Social Psychology, 37*, 1097-1126.

Faust, D. (1986). Research on human judgment and its application to clinical practice. *Professional Psychology: Research and Practice, 17*, 420-430.

Fensterheim, H., & Raw, S. D. (1996). Psychotherapy research is not psychotherapy practice. *Clinical Psychology: Science and Practice, 3*, 168-171.

Ferris, T. (1998). Not rocket science. *New Yorker, 74*, 4-5.

Fiese, B. H., Sameroff, A. J., Grotevant, H. D., Wamboldt, F. S., Dickstein, S., & Fravel, D. L. (2001). Observing families through the stories that they tell: A multidimensional approach. In P. Kerig & K. Lindahl (Eds.), *Family observational coding systems: Resources for systemic research* (pp. 259-271). Mahwah, NJ: Lawrence Erlbaum.

Fischer, J., & Corcoran, K. (1994). *Measures for clinical practice* (2nd ed.). New York: Free Press.

Foa, E. B., Grayson, J. B., Steketee, G. S., Doppelt, H. G., Turner, R. M., & Latimer, P. R. (1983). Success and failure in the behavioral treatment of obsessive-compulsives. *Journal of Consulting and Clinical Psychology, 51*, 287-297.

Frank, J. D., & Frank, J. B. (1991). *Persuasion and healing: A comparative study of psychotherapy* (3rd ed.). Baltimore, MD: Johns Hopkins University Press.

Fuhriman, A., & Burlingame, G. M. (1994). *Handbook of group psychotherapy.* New York: John Wiley.

Garb, H. N. (1992). The *trained* psychologist as expert witness. *Clinical Psychology Review, 12*, 451-467.

Garb, H. N. (1998). *Studying the clinician: Judgment research and psychological assessment.* Washington, DC: American Psychological Association.

Garb, H. N., Florio, C. M., & Grove, W. M. (1998). The validity of the Rorschach and the Minnesota Multiphasic Personality Inventory: Results from meta-analyses. *Psychological Science, 9*, 402-404.

Gentile, J. R. (1990). *Educational psychology.* Dubuque, IA: Kendall/Hunt.

Gladwell, M. (1996). Conquering the coma. *New Yorker, 72*, 34-40.

Goldman, L. (1972). Tests and counseling: The marriage that failed. *Measurement and Evaluation in Guidance, 15*, 70-73.

Goldman, L. (1992). Qualitative assessment: An approach for counselors. *Journal of Counseling & Development, 70*, 616-621.

Gottman, J. M. (1979). *Marital interaction: Experimental investigations.* New York: Academic Press.

Gottman, J. M., & Leiblum, S. R. (1974). *How to do psychotherapy and how to evaluate it.* New York: Holt, Rinehart & Winston.

Graham, J. R. (1990). *MMPI-2: Assessing personality and psychopathology.* New York: Oxford University Press.

Gray, G. V., & Lambert, M. J. (2001). Feedback: A key to improving therapy outcomes. *Behavioral Healthcare Tomorrow, 10*, 25-45.

Greenberg, L. S. (1986). Change process research. *Journal of Consulting and Clinical Psychology, 54*, 4-9.

Greene, G. J., Lee, M., Trask, R., & Rheinscheld, J. (2000). How to work with clients' strengths in crisis intervention: A solution-focused approach. In A. R. Roberts (Ed.), *Crisis intervention handbook: Assessment, treatment, and research* (2nd ed., pp. 31-55). New York: Oxford University Press.

Grieger, I., & Ponterotto, J. G. (1995). A framework for assessment in multicultural counseling. In J. G. Ponterotto, J. M. Casas, L. A. Suzuki, & C. M. Alexander (Eds.), *Handbook of multicultural counseling.* Thousand Oaks, CA: Sage.

Groth-Marnat, G. (1990). *Handbook of psychological assessment* (2nd ed.). New York: John Wiley.

Groth-Marnat, G. (2000). Visions of clinical assessment: Then, now, and a brief history of the future. *Journal of Clinical Psychology, 56*, 349-365.

Hanley, M. A. (2001). *A predictive model of health-related quality of life in obstructive sleep apnea patients.* Unpublished manuscript, State University of New York, Buffalo.

Hanna, F. J., Glordano, F. G., & Bemak, F. (1996). Theory and experience: Teaching dialectical thinking in counselor education. *Counselor Education and Supervision, 36*, 14-24.

Hartman, A. (1978). Diagrammatic assessment of family relationships. *Social Casework, 59*, 465-476.

Hartman, D. P. (1984). Assessment strategies. In D. H. Barlow & M. Hersen (Eds.), *Single case experimental designs* (pp. 107-139). New York: Pergamon.

Haverkamp, B. E. (1993). Confirmatory bias in hypothesis testing for client-identified and counselor self-generated hypotheses. *Journal of Counseling Psychology, 40*, 305-315.

Hayes, S. C. (1995). What do we want from scientific standards of psychological practice. In S. C. Hayes, V. M. Follette, R. M. Dawes, & K. E. Grady (Eds.), *Scientific standards of psychological practice: Issues and recommendations* (pp. 49-66). Reno, NV: Context.

Hayes, S. C., Barlow, D. H., & Nelson-Gray, R. O. (1999). *The scientist practitioner: Research and accountability in the age of managed care* (2nd ed.). Boston: Allyn & Bacon.

Hayes, S. C., Nelson, R. O., & Jarrett, R. B. (1987). The treatment utility of assessment. *American Psychologist, 42,* 963-974.

Haynes, S. N. (1993). Treatment implications of psychological assessment. *Psychological Assessment, 5,* 251-25.

Haynes, S. N. (2001). Introduction to the special section on clinical applications of analogue behavioral observation. *Psychological Assessment, 13,* 304.

Haynes, S. N., Spain, E. H., & Oliveira, J. (1993). Identifying causal relationships in clinical assessment. *Psychological Assessment, 5,* 281-291.

Henry, G. T. (1995). *Graphing data.* Thousand Oaks, CA: Sage.

Heppner, P. P., Carter, J. A., Claiborn, C. D., Brooks, L., Gelso, C. J., Fassinger, R. E., Holloway, E. L., Stone, G. L., Wampold, B. E., & Galassi, J. P. (1992). A proposal to integrate science and practice in counseling psychology. *The Counseling Psychologist, 20,* 107-122.

Heppner, P. P., Kivlighan, D. M., & Wampold, B. E. (1999). *Research design in counseling* (2nd ed.). Pacific Grove, CA: Brooks/Cole.

Hess, P. M., & Mullen, E. J. (1995). *Practitioner-researcher partnerships.* Washington, DC: NASW.

Heyman, R. E. (2001). Observation of couple conflicts: Clinical assessment applications, stubborn truths, and shaky foundations. *Psychological Assessment, 13,* 5-35.

Higgs, Z., & Gustafson, D. (1985). *Community as a client: Assessment and diagnosis.* Philadelphia: F. A. Davis.

Hill, C. E. (1982). Counseling process research: Philosophical and methodological dilemmas. *Counseling Psychologist, 10,* 7-19.

Hill, C. E. (1991). Almost everything you ever wanted to know about how to do process research on counseling and psychotherapy but didn't know who to ask. In C. Watkins & L. Schneider (Eds.), *Research in counseling* (pp. 85-118). Hillsdale, NJ: Lawrence Erlbaum.

Hoffman, B., & Meier, S. T. (2001). An individualized approach to managed mental health care in colleges and universities: A case study. *Journal of College Student Psychotherapy, 15,* 49-64.

Holland, J. L. (1997). *Making vocational choices: A theory of vocational personalities and work environments* (3rd ed.). Englewood Cliffs, NJ: Prentice Hall.

Holland, S. D., & Kendall, P. C. (1980). Cognitive self-statements in depression: Development of an Automatic Thoughts Questionnaire. *Cognitive Therapy and Research, 4,* 383-395.

Holloway, E. L. (1995). *Clinical supervision.* Thousand Oaks, CA: Sage.

Holloway, E. L., & Wolleat, P. L. (1980). Relationship of counselor conceptual level to clinical hypothesis formation. *Journal of Counseling Psychology, 27,* 539-545.

Hoshmand, L. T. (1994). *Orientation to inquiry in a reflective professional psychology.* Albany, NY: SUNY Press.

Howard, K. I., Brill, P. L., Lueger, R. J., & O'Mahoney, M. T. (1995). *Integra outpatient tracking system*. Philadelphia: Compass Information Services.

Howard, K. I., Kopta, S. M., Krause, M. S., & Orlinsky, D. E. (1986). The dose-effect relationship in psychotherapy. *American Psychologist, 41*, 159-164.

Howard, K. I., Lueger, R. J., Maling, M. S., & Martinovich, Z. (1993). A phase model of psychotherapy outcome: Causal mediation of change. *Journal of Consulting and Clinical Psychology, 61*, 678-685.

Howard, K. I., Moras, K., Brill, P. L., Martinovich, Z., & Lutz, W. (1996). Efficacy, effectiveness, and patient progress. *American Psychologist, 51*, 1059-1064.

Hoyle, R. H. (1999). *Statistical strategies for small sample research*. Thousand Oaks, CA: Sage.

Hser, Y.-I., Anglin, M. D., & Chou, C.-P. (1992). Reliability of retrospective self-report by narcotics addicts. *Psychological Assessment, 4*, 207-213.

Hummel, T. J. (1999). The usefulness of tests in clinical decisions. In J. W. Lichtenberg & R. K. Goodyear (Eds.), *Scientist-practitioner perspectives on test interpretation* (pp. 59-112). Needham Heights, MA: Allyn & Bacon.

Israeili, A. L., & Santor, D. A. (2000). Reviewing effective components of feminist therapy. *Counselling Psychology Quarterly, 13*, 233-247.

Iwakabe, S. (1999). Psychotherapy and chaos theory: The metaphoric relationship between psychodynamic therapy and chaos theory. *Psychotherapy, 36*, 274-286.

Jacobson, N. S., Schmaling, K. B., Holtzworth-Munroe, A., Katt, J. L., Wood, L. F., & Follette, V. M. (1989). Research structured vs. clinically flexible versions of social learning-based marital therapy. *Behaviour Research and Therapy, 27*, 173-180.

Joint Commission on Accreditation of Healthcare Organizations (JCAHO). (1997). *A practical guide to clinical documentation in behavioral health care*. Oakbrook Terrace, IL: Author.

Jones, E. E., Rock, L., Shaver, K. G., Goethals, G. R., & Ward, L. M. (1968). Pattern of performance and ability attribution: An unexpected primacy effect. *Journal of Personality and Social Psychology, 10*, 317-340.

Jongsma, A., & Peterson, L. (1995). *The compete psychotherapy treatment planner.* New York: John Wiley.

Jongsma, A., Peterson, L., & McInnis, W. (2001). *Therascribe 3.5* [Computer software]. New York: John Wiley.

Kadera, S. W., Lambert, M. J., & Andrews, A. A. (1996). How much therapy is really enough? *Journal of Psychotherapy Practice and Research, 5*, 132-151.

Kahn, J., & Meier, S. T. (1999). Level of measurement and the Family System Test: The relationship between participants' constructions and interpretation of scores. *Constructivism in the Human Sciences, 4*, 103-116.

Kahn, J., & Meier, S. T. (2001). Children's Definitions of Family Power and Cohesion Affect Scores on the Family System Test. *American Journal of Family Therapy, 29*, 141-154.

Kahn, J., & Scott, N. (1997). Predictors of research productivity and science-related career goals among counseling psychology doctoral students. *The Counseling Psychologist, 25*, 38-67.

Kahneman, D., Slovic, P., & Tversky, A. (Eds.). (1982). *Judgment under uncertainty: Heuristics and biases*. Cambridge, UK: Cambridge University Press.

Kanfer, F. H., & Schefft, B. K. (1988). *Guiding the process of therapeutic change*. Champaign, IL: Research.

Karasu, T. (1986). The specificity versus nonspecificity dilemma: Toward identifying therapeutic change agents. *American Journal of Psychiatry, 143*, 698-695.

Kaul, T. J., & Bednar, R. L. (1994). Pretraining and structure: Parallel lines yet to meet. In A. Fuhriman & G. M. Burlingame (Eds.), *Handbook of group psychotherapy*. New York: John Wiley.

Kazdin, A. E. (1980). *Research design in clinical psychology*. New York: Harper & Row.

Kazdin, A. E. (1993). Evaluation in clinical practice: Clinically sensitive and systematic methods of treatment delivery. *Behavior Therapy, 24*, 11-45.

Kazdin, A. E. (1999). Foreword. In P. W. Clement, *Outcomes and incomes* (pp. ix-xi). New York: Guilford.

Kelly, G. A. (1955). *The psychology of personal constructs* (Vols. 1-2). New York: Norton.

Kendall, P. C., Kipnis, D., & Otto-Salaj, L. (1992). When clients don't progress: Influences on and explanations of therapeutic progress. *Cognitive Therapy and Research, 16*, 269-281.

Kerig, P. (2001). Introduction and overview: Conceptual issues in family observational research. In P. Kerig & K. Lindahl (Eds.), *Family observational coding systems: Resources for systemic research* (pp. 1-22). Mahwah, NJ: Lawrence Erlbaum.

Kerig, P., & Lindahl, K. (Eds.). (2001). *Family observational coding systems: Resources for systemic research*. Mahwah, NJ: Lawrence Erlbaum.

Kessler, K. A. (1998). History of managed behavioral health care and speculations about its future. *Harvard Review of Psychiatry, 6*, 155-159.

Kilham, L. (1988). *On watching birds*. Chelsea, VT: Chelsea Green.

Kiresuk, T. J. (1994). Historical perspective. In T. J. Kiresuk, A. Smith, & J. E. Cardillo (Eds.), *Goal attainment scaling: Applications, theory, and measurement* (pp. 135-160). Hillsdale, NJ: Lawrence Erlbaum.

Kiresuk, T. J., Choate, R. O., Cardillo, J. E., & Larsen, N. (1994). Training in goal attainment scaling. In T. J. Kiresuk, A. Smith, & J. E. Cardillo (Eds.), *Goal attainment scaling: Applications, theory, and measurement* (pp. 105-118). Hillsdale, NJ: Lawrence Erlbaum.

Kiresuk, T. J., & Sherman, R. E. (1968). Goal attainment scaling: A general method for evaluating comprehensive community mental health programs. *Community Mental Health Journal, 4*, 443-453.

Kiresuk, T. J., Smith, A., & Cardillo, J. E. (1994). (Eds.). *Goal attainment scaling: Applications, theory, and measurement*. Hillsdale, NJ: Lawrence Erlbaum.

Kirschner, T., Hoffman, M., & Hill, C. E. (1994). Case study of the process and outcome of career counseling. *Journal of Counseling Psychology, 41*, 216-226.

Kopta, S. M., Howard, K. I., Lowry, J. L., & Beutler, L. E. (1994). Patterns of symptomatic recovery in psychotherapy. *Journal of Consulting & Clinical Psychology, 62*, 1009-1016.

Kozak, A. (1996). Local clinicians need knowledge tools. *American Psychologist, 51*, 1335-1336.

Krantz, D. H., Luce, R. D., Suppes, P., & Tversky, A. (1971). *Foundations of measurement: Vol. I. Additive and polynomial representations.* New York: Academic Press.

Lambert, M. J. (1994). Use of psychological tests for outcome assessment. In M. E. Maruish (Ed.), *The use of psychological testing for treatment planning and outcome assessment* (pp. 75-97). Hillsdale, NJ: Lawrence Erlbaum.

Lambert, M. J. (1998). Manual-based treatment and clinical practice: Hangman of life or promising development? *Clinical Psychology: Science & Practice, 5*, 391-395.

Lambert, M. J., & Huefner, J. C. (1996, August). *Measuring outcomes in clinical practice.* Workshop conducted at the American Psychological Association Annual Convention, Toronto.

Lambert, M. J., Whipple, J. L., Smart, D. W., Vermeesch, D. A., Nielsen, S. L., & Hawkins, E. J. (2001). The effects of providing therapists with feedback on patient progress during psychotherapy: Are outcomes enhanced? *Psychotherapy Research, 11*, 49-68.

Lambert, M. J., Whipple, J. L., Vermeesch, D. A., Smart, D. W., Hawkins, E. J., Nielsen, S. L., & Goates, M. (in press). Enhancing psychotherapy outcomes via providing feedback on client progress: A replication. *Journal of Consulting and Clinical Psychology.*

Lamiel, J. (1981). Toward an idiothetic psychology of personality. *American Psychologist, 36*, 276-289.

Lang, P. J. (1968). Fear reduction and fear behaviour: Problems in treating a construct. In J. M. Shlien (Ed.), *Research in psychotherapy* (Vol. 3, pp. 90-102). Washington, DC: American Psychological Association.

Langer, E. J., & Abelson, R. P. (1974). A patient by any other name . . . : Clinical group differences in labeling bias. *Journal of Consulting and Clinical Psychology, 42*, 4-9.

Lanyon, R. I., & Goodstein, L. D. (1982). *Personality assessment* (2nd ed.). New York: John Wiley.

Larson, E. B. (1999). N of 1 clinical trials—A technique for improving medical therapeutics. *Western Journal of Medicine, 152*, 52-56.

Layden, M., Newman, C., Freeman, A., & Morse, S. (1993). *Cognitive therapy of borderline personality disorder.* Needham Heights, MA: Allyn & Bacon.

Lazarus, A. A. (1997). *Brief but comprehensive psychotherapy: The multimodal way.* New York: Springer.

Leahy, R. L. (1999). Strategic self-limitation. *Journal of Cognitive Psychotherapy: An International Quarterly, 13*, 273-291.

Lee, T. M., Chen, E. Y., Chan, C. C., Paterson, J. G., Janzen, H. R., & Blashko, C. A. (1998). Seasonal Affective Disorder. *Clinical Psychology: Science & Practice, 5,* 275-290.

Lehman, D. R., Lempert, R. O., & Nisbett, R. E. (1988). The effects of graduate training on reasoning. *American Psychologist, 43,* 431-442.

Lewinsohn, P., & Rosenbaum, M. (1987). Recall of parental behavior by acute depressives, remitted depressives, and nondepressives. *Journal of Personality & Social Psychology, 52,* 611-619.

Lichstein, E. (1970). *Techniques for assessing outcomes of psychotherapy.* In P. McReynolds (Ed.), Advances in psychological assessment (Vol. 2, pp.178-197). Palo Alto, CA: Science and Behavior Books.

Licht, M. H., Paul, G. L., & Power, C. T. (1986). Standardized direct-multivariate DOC systems for service and research. In G. L. Paul (Ed.), *Assessment in residential treatment settings* (pp. 223-266). Champaign, IL: Research Press.

Lieberman, M., Yalom, I., & Miles, M. (1973). *Encounter groups: First facts.* New York: Basic Books.

Linehan, M. M. (1993). *Cognitive-behavioral treatment of borderline personality disorder.* New York: Guilford.

Lipsey, M. W. (1990). Theory as method: Small theories of treatments. In L. Sechrest, J. Bunker, & E. Perrin (Eds.), *Health services research methodology: Strengthening causal inference from nonexperimental research.* Washington, DC: U. S. Public Health Service, National Center for Health Services Research and Health Care Technology Research.

Lipsey, M. W., & Pollard, J. A. (1989). Driving toward theory in program evaluation: More models to choose from. *Evaluation and Program Planning, 12,* 317-328.

Loesch, L. C. (1977). Flow chart models for using tests. *Measurement and Evaluation in Guidance, 10,* 18-23.

Lueger, R. J. (1998). Using feedback on patient progress to predict the outcome of psychotherapy. *Journal of Clinical Psychology, 54,* 383-393.

Lyons, J., Howard, K., O'Mahoney, M., & Lish, J. (Eds.). (1997). *The measurement and management of clinical outcomes in mental health.* New York: John Wiley.

Lyons, T. F., & Payne, B. C. (1974). The relationship of physicians' medical recording performance to their medical care performance. *Medical Care, 12,* 463-469.

MacDonald, G. (1996). Inferences in therapy: Processes and hazards. *Professional Psychology: Research and Practice, 27,* 600-603.

Madill, A., Widdicombe, S., & Barkham, M. (2001). The potential of conversation analysis for psychotherapy research. *The Counseling Psychologist, 29,* 413-434.

Mahl, G. F. (1987). *Explorations in nonverbal and verbal behavior.* Hillsdale, NJ: Lawrence Erlbaum.

Malan, D. H. (1959). On assessing the results of psychotherapy. *British Journal of Medical Psychology, 32,* 86-105.

Maloney, M. P., & Ward, M. P. (1976). *Psychological assessment: A conceptual approach.* New York: Oxford University Press.

Mark, M., Rabinowitz, J., Kindler, S., Rabinowitz, S., Munitz, H., & Bleich, A. (1991). A system for improving psychiatric record keeping. *Hospital & Community Psychiatry, 42*, 1163-1166.

Martin, J., Slemon, A. G., Hiebert, B., Hallberg, E. T., & Cummings, A. L. (1989). Conceptualizations of novice and experienced counselors. *Journal of Counseling Psychology, 36*, 395-400.

Maruish, M. E. (1994). *The use of psychological testing for treatment planning and outcome assessment*. Hillsdale, NJ: Lawrence Erlbaum.

Mash, E. J. (1991). Measurement of parent-child interaction in studies of child maltreatment. In R. H. Starr, Jr. & D. A. Wolfe (Eds.), *The effects of child abuse and neglect* (pp. 203-256). New York: Guilford.

Mash, E. J., & Barkley, R. A. (1986). Assessment of family interaction with the Response-Class Matrix. In R. J. Prinz (Ed.), *Advances in the behavioral assessment of children and families* (pp. 29-69). Greenwich, CT: JAI.

Mash, E. J., & Foster, S. L. (2001). Exporting analogue behavioral observation from research to clinical practice: Useful or cost-defective? *Psychological Assessment, 13*, 86-98.

Mash, E. J., & Hunsley, J. (1993). Assessment considerations in the identification of failing psychotherapy: Bringing the negatives out of the darkroom. *Psychological Assessment, 5*, 292-301.

Masterpasqua, F., & Perna, P. A. (Eds). (1997). *The psychological meaning of chaos: Translating theory into practice*. Washington, DC: American Psychological Association.

Matarazzo, J. D. (1992). Psychological testing and assessment in the 21st century. *American Psychologist, 47*, 1007-1018.

Mattaini, M. A. (1993). *More than a thousand words: Graphics for clinical practice*. Washington, DC: NASW.

Mattaini, M. A. (1997). *Clinical practice with individuals*. Washington, DC: NASW Press.

Maxwell, J. A. (1996). *Qualitative research design: An interactive approach*. Thousand Oaks, CA: Sage.

McGuire, P. A. (1999). Multicultural summit cheers packed house. *APA Monitor, 30*, 26.

Meehl, P. E. (1954). *Clinical versus statistical prediction: A theoretical analysis and a review of the evidence*. Minneapolis: University of Minnesota Press.

Meichenbaum, D. H. (1980). Cognitive therapy modification. In C. H. Patterson (Ed.), *Theories of counseling psychotherapy* (3rd ed., pp. 251-270). New York: Harper & Row.

Meier, S. T. (1994). *The chronic crisis in psychological measurement and assessment*. New York: Academic Press.

Meier, S. T. (1997). Nomothetic item selection rules for tests of psychological interventions. *Psychotherapy Research, 7*, 419-427.

Meier, S. T. (1998). Evaluating change-based item selection rules. *Measurement and Evaluation in Counseling and Development, 31*, 15-27.

Meier, S. T. (1999). Training the practitioner-scientist: Bridging case conceptualization, assessment, and intervention. *The Counseling Psychologist, 27*, 589-613.

Meier, S. T., & Davis, S. R. (1990). Trends in reporting psychometric properties of instruments employed in counseling psychology research. *Journal of Counseling Psychology, 37*, 113-115.

Meier, S. T., & Davis, S. R. (2001). *The elements of counseling* (4th ed.). Pacific Grove, CA: Brooks/Cole.

Meier, S. T., & Letsch, E. (2000). Data collection issues in an urban community mental health center: What is necessary and sufficient information for outcome assessment? *Professional Psychology: Research and Practice, 31*, 409-411.

Meier, S. T., & Wick, M. (1991). Computer-based unobtrusive measurement: Potential supplements to reactive self-reports. *Professional Psychology: Research and Practice, 22*, 410-412.

Mergenthaler, E., & Kachele, H. (1996). Applying multiple computerized text-analytic measures to single psychotherapy cases. *Journal of Psychotherapy Practice & Research, 5*, 307-318.

Miles, M. B., & Huberman, A. M. (1994). *Qualitative data analysis.* Thousand Oaks, CA: Sage.

Mills, T. M. (1984). *The sociology of small groups* (2nd ed.). Englewood Cliffs, NJ: Prentice Hall.

Minuchin, S. (1974). *Families and family therapy.* Cambridge, MA: Harvard University Press.

Mori, L. T., & Armendariz, G. M. (2001). Analogue assessment of child behavior problems. *Psychological Assessment, 13*, 36-45.

Mossman, D. (1994). Assessing predictions of violence: Being accurate about accuracy. *Journal of Consulting and Clinical Psychology, 62*, 783-792.

Murdock, N. L. (1991). Case conceptualization: Applying theory to individuals. *Counselor Education and Supervision, 30*, 355-365.

Murphy, K. R., & Davidshofer, C. O. (1988). *Psychological testing.* Englewood Cliffs, NJ: Prentice Hall.

Murphy, K. R., & Davidshofer, C. O. (1994). *Psychological testing* (2nd ed.). Englewood Cliffs, NJ: Prentice Hall.

Nathan, P. E. (1998). Practice guidelines: Not yet ideal. *American Psychologist, 53*, 290-299.

Needleman, L. D. (1999). *Cognitive case conceptualization.* Mahwah, NJ: Lawrence Erlbaum.

Neimeyer, G. J. (1988). Cognitive integration and differentiation in vocational behavior. *The Counseling Psychologist, 16*, 440-475.

Neimeyer, G. J. (1989a). Application of repertory grid technique to vocational assessment. *Journal of Counseling and Development, 67*, 585-589.

Neimeyer, G. J. (1989b). Personal construct systems in vocational development and information-processing. *Journal of Career Development, 16*, 83-96.

Neimeyer, G. J., Brown, M. T., Metzler, A. E., Hagans, C., & Tanguy, M. (1989). The impact of sex, sex-role orientation, and construct type on vocational differentiation, integration, and conflict. *Journal of Vocational Behavior, 34*, 236-251.

Neimeyer, G. J., & Neimeyer, R. A. (1993). Defining the boundaries of constructivist assessment. In G. J. Neimeyer (Ed.), *Constructivist assessment* (pp. 1-30). Newbury Park, CA: Sage.

Neimeyer, R. A. (1993). Constructivist approaches to the measurement of meaning. In G. J. Neimeyer (Ed.), *Constructivist assessment* (pp. 58-103). Newbury Park, CA: Sage.

Nelson, M. L., & Neufeldt, S. A. (1998). The pedagogy of counseling: A critical examination. *Counselor Education and Supervision, 38*, 70-88.

Nelson, R. O. (1977a). Assessment and therapeutic functions of self-monitoring. In M. Hersen, R. M. Eisler, & P. M. Miller (Eds.), *Progress in behavior modification* (Vol. 5, pp. 263-308). New York: Brunner/Mazel.

Nelson, R. O. (1977b). Methodological issues in assessment via self-monitoring. In J. D. Cone & R. P. Hawkins (Eds.), *Behavioral assessment: New directions in clinical psychology* (pp. 217-254). New York: Brunner/Mazel.

Neufeld, R. W. J. (1977). *Clinical quantitative methods.* New York: Grune & Stratton.

Neufeldt, S. A., Iversen, J. N., & Juntunen, C. L. (1995). *Supervision strategies for the first practicum.* Alexandria, VA: American Counseling Association.

Neufeldt, S. A., Karno, M. P., & Nelson, M. L. (1996). A qualitative study of experts' conceptualization of supervisee reflectivity. *Journal of Counseling Psychology, 43*, 3-9.

Neville, H. A., & Mobley, M. (2001). Social identities in contexts: An ecological model of multicultural counseling psychology processes. *The Counseling Psychologist, 29*, 471-486.

Nezu, C., & Nezu, A. (1995). Clinical decision making in everyday practice: The science in the art. *Cognitive & Behavioral Practice, 2*, 5-25.

Nierenberg, A. A., & Mulroy, R. (1997). Declaration of treatment failures. In J. Rush (Ed.), *Mood disorders: Systematic medication management.* (Vol. 25, pp. 17-33). Basel, Switzerland: S. Karger AG.

Norcross, J. C., & Goldfried (Eds.). (1992). *Handbook of psychotherapy integration.* New York: Basic Books.

Norton, P. J., & Hope, D. A. (2001). Analogue observational methods in the assessment of social functioning in adults. *Psychological Assessment, 13*, 59-72.

Nugent, W. R., Sieppert, J. D., & Hudson, W. (2001). *Practice evaluation for the 21st Century.* Belmont, CA: Wadsworth.

Nunnally, J. C. (1967). *Psychometric theory.* New York: McGraw-Hill.

O'Brien, W. H. (1995). Inaccuracies in the estimation of functional relationships using self-monitoring data. *Journal of Behavior Therapy and Experimental Psychiatry, 26*, 351-357.

O'Donohue, W., & Elliott, A. N. (1991). A model for the clinical assessment of the sexually abuse child. *Behavioral Assessment, 13*, 325-339.

O'Donohue, W., Fisher, J. E., Plaud, J. J., & Link, W. (1989). What is a good treatment decision? The client's perspective. *Professional Psychology: Research and Practice, 20,* 404-407.

Ogles, B. M., Lambert, M. J., & Masters, K. S. (1996). *Assessing outcome in clinical practice.* Needham Heights, MA: Allyn & Bacon.

O'Neill, A. M. (1993). *Clinical inference: How to draw meaningful conclusions from tests.* Brandon, VT: Clinical Psychology.

Orlinsky, D. E., Grawe, K., & Parks, B. K. (1994). Process and outcome in psychotherapy: Noch einmal. In A. E. Bergin & S. L. Garfield (Eds.), *Handbook of psychotherapy and behavior change* (4th ed., pp. 270-376). New York, NY: John Wiley.

Palmer, R. H. (1986). Does quality assurance improve ambulatory care? Implementing a randomized controlled trial in sixteen group practices. *Journal of Ambulatory Care Management, 9,* 1-15.

Parker, K. C., Hanson, R. K., & Hunsley, J. (1988). MMPI, Rorschach and WAIS: A meta-analytic comparison of reliability, stability, and validity. *Psychological Bulletin, 103,* 367-373.

Parkinson, B., Briner, R., Reynolds, S., & Totterdell, P. (1995). Time frames for mood: Relations between monetary and generalized ratings of affect. *Personality & Social Psychology Bulletin, 21,* 331-339.

Patterson, C. H. (1996). Multicultural counseling: From diversity to universality. *Journal of Counseling & Development, 74,* 227-231.

Paul, G. L. (Ed.). (1986). *Assessment in residential treatment settings.* Champaign, IL: Research Press.

Paul, G. L. (1987a). *The time-sample behavioral checklist.* Champaign, IL: Research Press.

Paul, G. L. (Ed.). (1987b). *The staff-resident interaction chronograph.* Champaign, IL: Research Press.

Paul, G. L., Mariotto, M. J., & Redfield, J. P. (1986). Assessment purposes, domains, and utility for decision making. In G. L. Paul (Ed.), *Assessment in residential treatment settings* (pp. 1-26). Champaign, IL: Research Press.

Paul, G. L., & Menditto, A. A. (1992). Effectiveness of inpatient treatment programs for mentally ill adults in public psychiatric facilities. *Applied & Preventive Psychology, 1,* 41-63.

Pepinsky, H. B., & Pepinsky, N. (1954). *Counseling theory and practice.* New York: Ronald Press.

Persons, J. B. (1989). *Cognitive therapy in practice: A case formulation approach.* New York: Norton.

Persons, J. B., & Silberschaltz, G. (1998). Are results of randomized controlled trials useful to psychotherapists? *Journal of Consulting and Clinical Psychology, 66,* 126-135.

Pervin, L. (1984). Idiographic approaches to personality. In N. Endler & J. McV. Hunt (Eds.), *Personality and the behavioral disorders* (pp. 261-282). New York: John Wiley.

Peterson, D. R. (1992). Strategies of inquiry for the practice of psychology. *The Journal of Training and Practice in Professional Psychology, 6*, 35-45.

Peterson, R., McHolland, J., Bent, R., Davis-Russell, E., Edwall, G., Polite, K., Singer, D., & Stricker, G. (Eds.). (1991). *The core curriculum in professional psychology.* Washington, DC: American Psychological Association.

Piotrowski, C. (1996). Use of the Beck Depression Inventory in clinical practice. *Psychological Reports, 79*, 873-874.

Pitre, U., Dansereau, D. F., Newbern, D., & Simpson, D. D. (1998). Residential drug abuse treatment for probationers: Use of node-link mapping to enhance participation and progress. *Journal of Substance Abuse Treatment, 15*, 535-543.

Platt, J. R. (1977). Strong inference. In H. S. Broudy, R. H. Ennis, & L. I. Krimerman (Eds.), *Philosophy of educational research* (pp. 203-217). New York: John Wiley.

Prochaska, J. O. (1995). An eclectic and integrative approach: Transtheoretical therapy. In A. S. Gurman & S. B. Messer (Eds.), *Essential psychotherapies* (pp. 403-440). New York: Oxford University Press.

Prochaska, J. O., & DiClemente, C. C. (1983). Stages and processes of self-change in smoking: Toward an integrative model of change. *Journal of Consulting and Clinical Psychology, 5*, 390-395.

Quayle, M., & Moore, E. (1998). Evaluating the impact of structured groupwork with men in a high security hospital. *Criminal Behaviour and Mental Health, 8*, 77-92.

Rachman, S., & Hodgson, R. (1974). Synchrony and desynchrony in fear and avoidance. *Behavior Research and Therapy, 12*, 311-318.

Ridley, C., Li, L., & Hill, C. (1998). Multicultural assessment: Reexamination, reconceptualization, and practical application. *The Counseling Psychologist, 26*, 827-910.

Riskind, J. H., & Williams, N. L. (1999). Dynamic cognitive case conceptualization and the treatment of anxiety disorders: Implications of the looming vulnerability model. *Journal of Cognitive Psychotherapy: An International Quarterly, 13*, 293-313.

Robbins, M. S., Hervis, O., Mitrani, V. B., & Szapocznik, J. (2001). Assessing changes in family interaction: Structural Family Systems Ratings. In P. Kerig & K. Lindahl (Eds.), *Family observational coding systems: Resources for systemic research* (pp. 207-224). Mahwah, NJ: Lawrence Erlbaum.

Roberts, M. W. (2001). Clinic observations of structured parent-child interaction designed to evaluate externalizing disorders. *Psychological Assessment, 13*, 46-58.

Rollock, D., & Terrell, M. (1996). Multicultural issues in assessment: Toward an inclusive model. In J. DeLucia-Waack (Ed.), *Multicultural counseling competencies: Implications for training and practice* (pp. 113-153). Alexandria, VA: Association for Counselor Education and Supervision.

Ronnestad, M., & Skovholt, T. (2001). Learning arenas for professional development: Retrospective accounts of senior psychotherapists. *Professional Psychology: Research & Practice, 32*, 181-187.

Rosen, A. (1992). Facilitating clinical decision making and evaluation. *Families in Society: The Journal of Contemporary Human Services, 73*, 522-532.

Saal, F. E., Downey, R. G., & Lahey, M. A. (1980). Rating the ratings: Assessing the psychometric quality of rating data. *Psychological Bulletin, 88*, 413-428.

Sandifer, M., Hordern, A., & Green, L. (1970). The psychiatric interview: The impact of the first three minutes. *American Journal of Psychiatry, 126*, 968-973.

Sarbin, T. R. (1986). Prediction and clinical inference: Forty years later. *Journal of Personality Assessment, 50*, 362-369.

Schulte, D., Kunzel, R., Pepping, G., & Schulte-Bahrenberg, T. (1992). Tailor-made versus standardized therapy of phobic patients. *Advances in Behaviour Research and Therapy, 14*, 67-92.

Schwarz, N. (1999). Self-reports: How the questions shape the answers. *American Psychologist, 54*, 93-105.

Schwitzer, A. M. (1996). Using the inverted pyramid heuristic in counselor education and supervision. *Counselor Education & Supervision, 35*, 258-267.

Shadel, W. G., Niaura, R., & Abrams, D. B. (2000). An idiographic approach to understanding personality structure and individual differences among smokers. *Cognitive Therapy and Research, 24*, 345-359.

Silverman, M., Ricci, E., & Gunter, M. (1990). Strategies for increasing the rigor of qualitative methods in evaluation of health care programs. *Evaluation Review, 14*, 57-74.

Skovholt, T., & Ronnestad, M. (1995). *The evolving professional self: Stages and themes in therapist and counselor development.* New York: John Wiley.

Smith, M. L., & Glass, G. V. (1977). Meta-analysis of psychotherapy outcome studies. *American Psychologist, 32*, 752-760.

Snyder, M., & Swann, W. B., Jr. (1978). Hypothesis-testing processes in social interaction. *Journal of Personality and Social Psychology, 36*, 1202-1212.

Sommers-Flanagan, J., & Sommers-Flanagan, R. (1999). *Clinical interviewing* (2nd ed.). Needham Heights, MA: Allyn & Bacon.

Speer, D. C., & Newman, F. L. (1996). Mental health services outcome evaluation. *Clinical Psychology: Science & Practice, 3*, 105-129.

Spengler, P. M., & Strohmer, D. C. (1994). Clinical judgment biases: The moderating roles of counselor cognitive complexity and counselor client preferences. *Journal of Counseling Psychology, 41*, 8-17.

Spengler, P. M., Strohmer, D. C., Dixon, D. N., & Shivy, V. A. (1995). A scientist-practitioner model of psychological assessment: Implications for training, practice and research. *The Counseling Psychologist, 23*, 506-534.

Sperry, L., Brill, P. L., Howard, K. I., & Grissom, G. R. (1996). *Treatment outcomes in psychotherapy and psychiatric interventions.* New York: Brunner/Mazel.

Spielberger, C. D., Gorsuch, R. L., & Lushene, R. (1970). *Manual for the State-Trait Anxiety Inventory: STAI.* Palo Alto, CA: Consulting Psychologists Press.

Stiles, W. B. (1980). Measurement of the impact of psychotherapy sessions. *Journal of Consulting and Clinical Psychology, 48*, 176-185.

Stoltenberg, C. D., Kashubeck-West, S., Biever, J. L., Patterson, T., & Welch, D. (2000). Training models in counseling psychology: Scientist-practitioner versus practitioner-scholar. *The Counseling Psychologist, 28*, 622-640.

Stoltenberg, C. D., McNeill, B., & Delworth, U. (1998). *IDM supervision.* San Francisco: Jossey-Bass.

Strack, F., Schwarz, N., & Gschneidinger, E. (1985). Happiness and reminiscing: The role of time perspective, mood, and mode of thinking. *Journal of Personality and Social Psychology, 49,* 1460-1469.

Strauss, A., & Corbin, J. (Eds.). (1997). *Grounded theory in practice.* Thousand Oaks, CA: Sage.

Streiner, D. L. (1998). Thinking small: Research designs appropriate for clinical practice. *Canadian Journal of Psychiatry, 43,* 737-741.

Stricker, G., & Trierweiler, S. J. (1995). The local clinical scientist: A bridge between science and practice. *American Psychologist, 50,* 995-1002.

Strong, S. R. (1995). Interpersonal influence theory: The situational and individual determinants of interpersonal behavior. In D. J. Lubinski & R. V. Dawis (Eds.), *Assessing individual differences in human behavior: New concepts, methods, and findings* (pp. 263-295). Palo Alto, CA: Consulting Psychologists.

Strong, S. R., Welsh, J. A., Corcoran, J. L., & Hoyt, W. T. (1992). Social psychology and counseling psychology: The history, products, and promise of an interface. *Journal of Counseling Psychology, 39,* 139-157.

Strupp, H. H., & Anderson, T. (1997). On the limitations of therapy manuals. *Clinical Psychology: Science and Practice, 4,* 76-82.

Strupp, H. H., Horowitz, L. M., & Lambert, M. J. (Eds.). (1997). *Measuring patient changes in mood, anxiety, and personality disorders: Toward a core battery.* Washington, DC: American Psychological Association.

Sue, D. W., Ivey, A. E., & Pedersen, P. B. (Eds.). (1996). *A theory of multicultural counseling and therapy.* Pacific Grove, CA: Brooks/Cole.

Swenson, E. V., & Ragucci, R. (1984). Effects of sex-role stereotypes and androgynous alternatives on mental health judgments of psychotherapists. *Psychological Reports, 54,* 475-481.

Teyber, E. (2000). *Interpersonal process in psychotherapy* (4th ed.). Pacific Grove, CA: Brooks/Cole.

Tompkins, M. A. (1999). Using case formulation to manage treatment nonresponse. *Journal of Cognitive Psychotherapy: An International Quarterly, 13,* 317-331.

Tracey, T. J., & Rounds, J. (1999). Inference and attribution errors in test interpretation. In J. W. Lichtenberg & R. K. Goodyear (Eds.), *Scientist-practitioner perspectives on test interpretation* (pp. 59-112). Needham Heights, MA: Allyn & Bacon.

Tracey, T. J., Ellickson, J. L., & Sherry, P. (1989). Reactance in relation to different supervisory environments and counselor development. *Journal of Counseling Psychology, 36,* 336-344.

Trierweiler, S. J., & Stricker, G. (1998). *The scientific practice of professional psychology.* New York: Plenum.

Tufte, E. R. (1983). *Visual display of quantitative information.* Cheshire, CT: Graphics.

Tufte, E. R. (1990). *Envisioning information.* Cheshire, CT: Graphics.

Tukey, J. W. (1977). *Exploratory data analysis*. Reading, MA: Addison-Wesley.

Twentyman, C., Boland, T., & McFall, R. M. (1981). Heterosexual avoidance in college males. *Behavior Modification, 5*, 523-552.

VandenBos, G. R. (1996). Outcome assessment of psychotherapy. *American Psychologist, 51*, 1005-1106.

Velicer, W. F., Rossi, J. S., Prochaska, J. O., & DiClemente, C. C. (1996). A criterion measurement model for health behavior change. *Addictive Behaviors, 21*, 555-584.

Viglione, D. J. (1999). A review of recent research addressing the utility of the Rorschach. *Psychological Assessment, 11*, 251-265.

Vogt, W. P. (1999). *Dictionary of statistics and methodology: A nontechnical guide for the social sciences* (2nd ed.). Thousand Oaks, CA: Sage.

Wampold, B. E. (2001). *The great psychotherapy debate: Models, methods, and findings*. Mahwah, NJ: Lawrence Erlbaum.

Wantz, D., & Morran, D. (1994). Teaching counselor trainees a divergent versus a convergent hypothesis-formation strategy. *Journal of Counseling & Development, 73*, 69-73.

Watkins, C. E., Jr. (1997). Some concluding thoughts about psychotherapy supervision. In C. E. Watkins, Jr. (Ed.), *Handbook of psychotherapy supervision* (pp. 603-616). New York: John Wiley.

Webb, E., Campbell, D., Schwartz, R., Sechrest, L., & Grove, J. (1981). *Nonreactive measures in the social sciences*. Boston: Houghton Mifflin.

Wedding, D., & Faust, D. (1989). Clinical judgment and decision making in neuropsychology. *Archives of Clinical Neuropsychology, 4*, 233-265.

Weisz, J. R., Weiss, B., Han, S. S., Granger, D. A., & Morton, T. (1995). Effects of psychotherapy with children and adolescents revisited: A meta-analysis of treatment outcome studies. *Psychological Bulletin, 177*, 450-468.

Weizenbaum, J. (1976). *Computer power and human reason*. San Francisco: Freeman.

Westen, D., & Morrison, K. (2001). A multi-dimensional meta-analysis of treatments for depression, panic, and generalized anxiety disorder: An empirical examination of the status of empirically supported therapies. *Journal of Consulting and Clinical Psychology, 69*, 875-899.

Wiger, D. (1999). *The psychotherapy documentation primer*. New York: John Wiley.

Wiggins, J. S. (1973). *Personality and prediction: Principles of personality assessment*. Reading, MA: Addison-Wesley.

Wiley, D. (1991). Test validity and invalidity reconsidered. In R. E. Snow & E. Wiley (Eds.), *Improving inquiry in social science* (pp. 75-108). Hillsdale, NJ: Lawrence Erlbaum.

Wilson, G. T. (1996). Manual-based treatments: The clinical application of research findings. *Behavior Research and Therapy, 34*, 295-314.

Yalom, I. (1995). *Theory and practice of group psychotherapy* (4th ed.). New York: Basic Books.

Ziskin, J. Z. (1995). *Coping with psychiatric and psychological testimony* (5th ed.). Los Angeles: Law and Psychology Press.

Zuckerman, E. L. (1997). *The paper office* (2nd ed.). New York: Guilford.

INDEX

⊰ ONE ⊱

ABOUT THE AUTHOR

Scott T. Meier is Professor and Co-Director of Training of the Program in Counseling/School Psychology, Department of Counseling, School, and Educational Psychology, University at Buffalo. His major research and teaching areas focus on psychological assessment and testing (particularly outcome assessment), research methods (particularly program evaluation), and counseling skills (particularly the integration of case conceptualization and assessment with intervention). He is a licensed psychologist who received his Ph.D. in Counseling Psychology from Southern Illinois University, Carbondale in 1984. He is also the author or coauthor of four books, including *Elements of Counseling* (Brooks/Cole, 2001), and 40 journal articles.